I0783370

WOKE II

THE SEQUEL NOBODY WANTED, BUT EVERYONE NEEDS

MAXIMUM EFFORT

CHAPTER ONE PUBLISHING COMPANY, LLC.

Copyright © 2024 by **Maximum Effort Productions**

All rights reserved.

No part of this publication may be reproduced, distributed, or transmitted in any form or by any means, including photocopying, recording, or other electronic or mechanical methods, without the prior written permission of the publisher, except in the case of brief quotations used in book reviews or critical analyses.

Maximum Effort Productions is a registered trademark with the U.S. Copyright Office.

Legal Notice

This publication is protected under copyright law. Unauthorized duplication, distribution, or reproduction of any content within this book is strictly prohibited and punishable by law. Any use of this content without explicit permission is a violation of copyright and intellectual property rights.

Moral Rights

The author asserts the moral right to be identified as the creator of this work.

Trademarks

All trademarks, product names, and logos used in this publication are the property of their respective owners. Reference to any product, service, or company is for informational purposes only and does not constitute endorsement or sponsorship.

Disclaimer

This book is intended for educational and entertainment purposes only. While every effort has been made to ensure the accuracy and completeness of the information presented, the author and publisher disclaim any liability for errors, omissions, or inconsistencies. This book does not provide legal, financial, medical, or professional advice. Readers are encouraged to seek the assistance of a licensed professional before acting on any information contained herein.

By reading this book, the reader agrees that the author and publisher are not liable for any direct, indirect, incidental, or consequential damages resulting from the use or misuse of the information provided.

External Content

The publisher does not guarantee the accuracy or availability of any third-party websites or references mentioned in this book and assumes no responsibility for their content.

CONTENTS

~

DEDICATION

~

- To every HR manager who thinks their beige PowerPoint presentation on "Workplace Accountability" is going to change lives—this is your nightmare in hardcover. To every compliance officer who lives for sending those soul-crushing "just a friendly reminder" emails at 4:59 PM on a Friday—your reign of terror ends here. This one's for you.

- To the Twitter mobbers with their caps-locked outrage, who can't wait to unleash their "ratio" on anyone who dares to think independently—don't worry, you'll get your dopamine hit soon enough. You're not warriors of justice. You're glorified hall monitors with Wi-Fi.

- To the easily offended, the perpetually triggered, and the ones who've made pearl-clutching their full-time job—strap in because this book will have you Googling "safe space" by page five. Your outrage is free marketing, and your tears? Pure gold

- To the self-righteous pretentious influencers who love posting 12-minute apology videos for clout: keep crying on camera and cashing those ad revenue checks. You've mastered the art of fake remorse better than a politician in a sex scandal. Bravo.

- To the keyboard warriors with "unacceptable" on auto-type and the ones who proudly wield the phrase "do better" like a sword, the irony of you needing to touch grass is almost poetic.

- To everyone who loves to call out "problematic" people while quietly scrubbing their own skeleton-filled closets —don't worry, I brought receipts.

- To the people who believe their feelings are facts: buckle up. You're about to feel every single word of this book like a slap across your participation-trophy face. **Spoiler:** you're not unique, and neither are your feelings. No One gives a fuck about you.

- To every "thought leader" who thinks their LinkedIn post about "embracing vulnerability" is profound— you're as inspiring as wet cardboard. Nobody cares about your "journey to authenticity" or your third attempt at a side hustle that you'll abandon in six months.

- To the sanctimonious warriors of cancel culture: your entire existence is a parody. You're not "speaking truth to power"—you're just bored - get a life. Your hashtags hold as much weight as a politician's empty promises, and your callouts? Whispered into the void.

- To every brand that's ever groveled in a public apology over a tweet no one remembered five minutes later: congrats on being the corporate equivalent of a limp dick. You've proven that nothing screams "integrity" like bending over backward for the internet's approval.

- To the Gen Z activists who think they're reinventing the wheel by yelling about things the rest of us solved decades ago: it must be exhausting being this performative. **Pro tip:** your "activism" ends where your Wi-Fi signal does.

- To every HR policy designed to suck the life out of the workplace—consider this book my two weeks' notice to your bullshit.

- To every "accountability advocate" who loves to tweet about "holding people responsible" while ducking accountability for their own messes: congratulations, you've become the clowns you claim to hate.

- To the people who cancel comedians for jokes: here's a concept that'll blow your fragile little minds—comedy isn't about making you feel safe. If you don't like the joke, don't laugh. It's not rocket science, but then again, thinking clearly has never been your strong suit.

- To the self-appointed empathy police: spare me. Your version of "compassion" is as authentic as your Instagram filters.

- To every online troll who gets a stiff one from ruining someone's day: you're not clever, you're just a sad little parasite looking for validation in a comment thread. I hope this book makes you cry.

- To the people who confuse virtue signaling with actual virtue: you're not heroes, you're hypocrites. Your outrage is performative, your activism is lazy, and your hashtags mean less than a New Year's resolution by January 3rd.

- To the corporate overlords who fire employees for tweets from a decade ago—may your stock price plummet and your PR team quit en masse.

- To every person who's ever said, "We need to do better," without an ounce of irony: you first, you dumb ass idiots.

- To the sanctimonious souls who spend their days scrolling social media looking for someone to destroy: find a hobby. Take up knitting, learn a language, or stare at a wall—anything is better than the pathetic existence you're clinging to now.

- To the phrase "This is not who we are,": yes, it is. Stop lying.

- To every college admissions officer who spends more time analyzing TikTok accounts than transcripts: you're everything wrong with the world, wrapped in a suit and tie.

- To the "brave" internet warriors who call themselves whistleblowers while hiding behind anonymous accounts: you're about as courageous as a cat in a thunderstorm.

- To the professional victims who thrive on outrage, your entire existence is a walking punchline.

- And finally, to the unbothered—the ones who sip their coffee, scroll past the drama, and live rent-free in the heads of the perpetually offended—this book is your anthem.

This isn't an olive branch. It's a flamethrower. Consider this your warning.

∾

If this dedication makes you mad, the rest of the book will break you.

∾

INTRODUCTION

Welcome to Hell. Population: You.

Congratulations, dumbass. You opened this book. That's your first mistake. Closing it would've been smarter—hell, curling up in a corner with a glass of warm milk and reading your HR compliance manual would've been a better use of your time. But no, here you are, willingly stepping into the chaos with the grace of a drunk toddler on roller skates.

Let me make this crystal fucking clear: this isn't a self-help book. This isn't a "safe space." And it sure as hell isn't some kumbaya circle where we hold hands, cry about the state of the world, and hope the power of positivity saves us. If that's what you're looking for, do yourself a favor and slam this book shut. Hell, light it on fire for all I care. At least then you'd have done something bold for once in your life.

This is **Maximum Fucking Effort**—and we're here to torch every sacred cow grazing on the fields of modern idiocy. No apologies, no hand-holding, and definitely no fucks given.

If you're easily offended, now's the time to bail. Seriously. Rip off the Band-Aid, toss this book into the nearest dumpster, and go do whatever fragile people like you do to soothe your egos. Knit a blanket. Hug your emotional support cactus. Write a tweet about how this book hurt your feelings. Just don't keep reading.

But if you're still here—if you're one of the few who can stomach the truth—you're in for one hell of a ride.

~

Welcome to WOKE WORLD 2.0

Absurdity isn't just tolerated anymore—it's celebrated. This is WOKE WORLD 2.0, a dystopia so riddled with contradictions and insanity that Orwell himself would throw up his hands and say, *"I didn't sign up for this."*

Imagine your kid coming home and announcing they now identify as "species-fluid." Suddenly, little Johnny is Meow Meow, the Cat, and the school—terrified of a viral TikTok callout—has installed litter boxes in the bathrooms. That's not a joke—it's the world we live in. This isn't satire. This is reality being run through a fucking meat grinder of delusion.

Or picture your office banning water cooler conversations altogether because "hydration zones reinforce workplace hierarchies." Forget that you just wanted to talk about last night's game—

now you're guilty of committing "nonverbal microaggressions" against Karen from Accounting.

And WOKE isn't just in schools or offices. Oh no, champ. It's in your cereal aisle, your Netflix recommendations, and even your damn emojis. Post the wrong GIF, and suddenly you're ableist. Use the thumbs-up emoji, and congratulations—you're now "aggressively passive-aggressive." Humor is now a minefield, individuality is a crime, and logic has been shot execution-style in the back of the head.

The mob doesn't just want compliance—they want blood. And the more you give, the hungrier they get.

～

What the Hell Happened to Us?

How did we get here? When did we decide to give participation trophies to kids who couldn't tie their own fucking shoes? When did HR departments start neutering workplaces, banning normal human interactions, and turning break rooms into minefields of microaggressions?

No, it wasn't just that. It was the internet. The internet took everything wrong with humanity—pettiness, narcissism, and an insatiable hunger for validation—and pumped it full of steroids. Suddenly, every idiot with a keyboard had a megaphone, and instead of saying something meaningful, we used it to scream about which Marvel movie had the best post-credits scene.

Outrage became the currency of the realm. Likes, retweets, ratios—these are the new metrics of morality. We don't solve problems anymore; we perform them. We don't debate; we cancel. And somehow, through all this chaos, we convinced ourselves that we're the good guys. Spoiler alert: we're not.

~

Maximum Effort's War Cry

This book isn't for everyone. If you're looking for comfort, validation, or some bullshit participation trophy, close this book and go meditate with your emotional support rock. This isn't your safe space.

This is a war cry. A flamethrower aimed at every smug, self-righteous asshole who thinks their hashtags make them heroes. This is the middle finger to a world that's forgotten how to laugh, how to think, how to take a fucking joke without crying into their $8 soy lattes.

I'm not here to apologize. Not for my opinions. Not for my language. And definitely not for hurting your feelings. If you're offended, good. Offense is the wake-up call most people are too cowardly to answer.

~

Taking Back Sanity

You don't have to play along. You don't have to tiptoe around absurd rules or grovel for the mob. This book isn't just a critique—

it's a survival guide. By the end of this journey, you'll know how to log off, stop apologizing, and take back your life.

You'll learn how to laugh at the madness, call out the hypocrisy, and maybe—just maybe—rediscover what it means to be free.

~

Closing Line: The War Starts Now

You've made it this far, and now you have a choice: resist or comply. This isn't just a book—it's your battle cry.

So turn the page, and let's set this shit circus on fire. Together, we'll torch every sacred cow, topple every soapbox, and burn this dystopian hellscape to the ground. And when we're done? Maybe, just maybe, we'll start rebuilding something worth saving.

Are you ready? Good. Now let's fucking go.

~

CHAPTER 1

WELCOME TO WOKE WORLD — THE ONBOARDING OF YOUR NIGHTMARES

"Sign here. Shut up. And remember, silence is violence."

~

Welcome to the Machine

The room hums with the oppressive glow of LED lights, a soulless hum that sets the stage for what can only be described as your induction into madness. You step through the frosted glass doors clutching a welcome packet the size of a dictionary. The receptionist—no, scratch that, the "Inclusivity Gatekeeper"—sits behind a desk adorned with signs that read: *Empathy is Mandatory, Inclusion Without Limits,* and the truly ominous, *Your Pronouns. Your Future.*

THE GATEKEEPER EYES you like you just coughed in a vegan cafe. "Sign in here," they say, sliding over a tablet covered in pastel banners and

19

rotating emojis. A flashing prompt demands: *Declare Your Pronouns Before Proceeding.*

You hesitate. Big mistake.

"Are you hesitating?" The Gatekeeper's tone drips with disdain, like you just insulted their gluten-free croissant. The room goes silent. A bead of sweat forms on your forehead.

"Uh... he/him," you stammer. Relief washes over you—briefly.

The Gatekeeper's smile is sharp enough to cut glass. "Brave choice. But remember, that's only valid until tomorrow." They slap a lanyard around your neck. The digital badge glows with your new identity: *Subject 427: He/Him. Valid Until Midnight.*

Welcome to WOKE WORLD.

~

HR: Humanity Reprogrammed

HR isn't "Human Resources" anymore. That's too narrow, too limiting, and far too human. They've rebranded as *Harmony Regulators.* Their mission? To ensure emotional compliance at all costs. Forget payroll or benefits—they now manage your soul.

· · ·

THE ONBOARDING SESSION begins with a hologram of the Chief Inclusivity Officer, a figure who looks like a hybrid of Oprah, Elon Musk, and your high school principal. "Welcome, new team member!" the hologram booms with televangelist fervor. "Here at WOKE WORLD, we prioritize emotional safety over productivity. Remember: Your work matters less than your words, and your words matter less than your intentions."

THE HOLOGRAM PAUSES, scanning the room as if it can see directly into your thoughts. "Any deviation will result in corrective empathy training."

YOU GLANCE NERVOUSLY at the person next to you. They lean in and whisper, "Corrective empathy training is a three-day simulation where you live as a trending Twitter hashtag. People say you never come back the same."

~

Mandatory Empathy Audits

AT FIRST GLANCE, the **Empathy Band** seems innocuous—a sleek gadget promising to "promote workplace harmony." But within minutes, it reveals its true nature: a high-tech snitch designed to measure compliance with the unspoken laws of emotional servitude.

Scenario 1: The Smirk of Doom

You're sitting in a mandatory workshop titled *"Unpacking Privilege Through Interpretive Dance."* The instructor, a self-proclaimed Empathy Guru, begins a performance that looks like a cross between modern ballet and a toddler's tantrum. You stifle a smirk—a reflex, not rebellion.

Big mistake.

The Empathy Band lights up, its sensors detecting the subtle curl of your lip. A warning shock jolts your wrist, not enough to cause pain but enough to remind you that dissent—even silent dissent—is unacceptable. Your heart races, spiking your "Empathy Stress Level" into the yellow zone. On the wall, a public leaderboard flashes:

- **Subject 427**: EMPATHY SCORE 78% (AT RISK)

Gasps echo around the room. You're now a pariah. The facilitator pauses mid-leap to glare at you. "Is there something you'd like to share, Subject 427? Perhaps an apology for your micro-expression of disdain?"

You nod furiously, stammering an apology while the band buzzes with approval. Your score inches back to 80%, but the damage is done. You're now flagged for a follow-up *Empathy Review Session*.

Scenario 2: The Silent Rebellion

IT'S 3:00 PM, and you're trapped in a Zoom meeting called *"Species Fluidity in the Workplace: A Primer."* Your camera is on—mandatory, of course—and the presenter drones on about the importance of providing amphibian-friendly office spaces.

YOU BLINK. That's all. A slow blink.

THE EMPATHY BAND interprets it as boredom, setting off a subtle vibration on your wrist. Your reflection stares back at you from the Zoom screen, wide-eyed and forced into a frozen, over-attentive expression. But it's too late. The presenter's screen flickers as your *Micro-Expression Deficiency Alert* is broadcast to all attendees.

"SUBJECT 427, your Empathy Score has dropped to 74%. Would you like to explain why this topic doesn't seem to resonate with you?"

EVERYONE STARES. You stumble through a response about the importance of inclusivity for frogs, turtles, and salamanders, desperately willing your band to stop buzzing. It doesn't. By the end of the meeting, your score is a dismal 68%, and an auto-generated email lands in your inbox:

Subject: Reflective Accountability Taskforce Appointment

ATTENDANCE IS MANDATORY. Prepare a 1,000-word essay on "Why I Failed to Empathize with Non-Human Identities."

. . .

Scenario 3: The Hugging Debacle

IT'S CASUAL FRIDAY, and the office is hosting a *"Mandatory Empathy Team-Building Event."* You're forced to join a group exercise called *"Unconditional Emotional Affirmations Through Contact."* Translation: awkward hugs with coworkers.

YOUR TURN COMES, and you reluctantly embrace Todd from Finance, who insists on identifying as "warm and cuddly." The Empathy Band scans your vitals—heart rate too steady, body temperature too low. The band interprets your lack of nervous sweat as a lack of connection.

"SUBJECT 427," the facilitator chirps. "Your Empathy Score indicates insufficient warmth. Would you like to try again?"

YOU GRIMACE, hugging Todd tighter while internally screaming. But your band still doesn't approve. It pings loudly, triggering a room-wide notification:

SUBJECT 427 EMPATHY DEFICIENCY: Group Hug Failure Detected.

THE ROOM ERUPTS IN MURMURS. You're now on the **Empathy**

Watchlist, a status that bars you from using the coffee machine or sitting in the prime corner office spots.

The Reflective Accountability Taskforce (RAT): A Tribunal of Shame

By the end of the week, you find yourself in the RAT chamber—a sterile, windowless room where your coworkers sit in judgment.

"Subject 427," the lead facilitator begins, her voice dripping with faux compassion. "Your empathy deficits have disrupted the emotional ecosystem of this workplace. How do you plead?"

It's a kangaroo court where every apology sounds like a confession and every defense is twisted into further proof of guilt. By the time the tribunal ends, you're sentenced to **Corrective Empathy Training**—three days in a virtual reality simulation where you experience life as a sentient hashtag under relentless public scrutiny.

As you leave the chamber, your Empathy Band pings with a chilling notification:

"Remember: Emotional Safety Is Everyone's Responsibility."

THE MESSAGE IS CLEAR: Step in line, or step aside. Welcome to the nightmare.

~

Pronoun Roulette

EVERY 12 HOURS, the spinning wheel of progressivism resets your identity. It's no longer just a game of personal expression—it's a corporate mandate designed to test your memory, compliance, and willpower to survive. At the stroke of midnight and noon, the **Inclu-siVibe** app pings with a cheerful notification:

"CONGRATULATIONS, Subject 427! Your new pronouns are ze/zir. Reminder: Failure to use updated pronouns may result in immediate disciplinary action."

BUT DON'T LET the chirpy tone fool you. This isn't a suggestion. It's a trap.

Scenario 1: The Morning Mishap

IT'S 8:00 AM, and you're rushing to your first meeting. Your coffee hasn't kicked in, and you accidentally refer to Chloe from marketing —whose pronouns were she/her last cycle—as they/them. Chloe gasps audibly, her Empathy Band lighting up like a Christmas tree.

. . .

"Excuse me, Subject 427," Chloe snaps, holding up her lanyard where the new pronouns **ae/aer** flash in bold letters. "Did you just mispronoun me?"

You stammer an apology, but it's too late. The room falls silent as everyone's InclusiVibe app buzzes with an alert:

Pronoun Violation Detected: Subject 427. Empathy Score Deduction: -15 Points.

The deduction is instantaneous. Your name on the company leaderboard plummets into the red zone, flashing a warning to all: *PROBLEMATIC BEHAVIOR DETECTED.* Chloe smirks, basking in the righteous glow of victimhood.

Scenario 2: The Lunchroom Trap

You're in the cafeteria, starving and hoping to grab a quick bite. But the line at the sandwich station is a minefield of pronoun etiquette. Each employee's badge displays their ever-shifting pronouns, and the tension is palpable.

You step up to the counter, nodding at Alex, the sandwich artist. "Can I get a turkey wrap, please?"

. . .

Alex's face darkens. "Did you even check my pronouns?" They—or rather **it/its**—points furiously at their badge.

You freeze, realizing you forgot to scan the Pronoun Board at the entrance. Your Empathy Band buzzes violently as the cafeteria PA system announces:

"Subject 427 has failed to respect inclusivity protocols. Empathy Score Deduction: -30 Points. Restricted access to coffee machine activated."

The lunch line grumbles as you're escorted out, leaving your appetite—and dignity—behind.

Scenario 3: The Quarterly Pronoun Quiz

Every quarter, employees are required to pass the **Pronoun Proficiency Assessment**—a rigorous, timed quiz testing your ability to recall every coworker's pronouns over the past three months. Forgetting even one detail results in public shaming.

You sit nervously in front of the screen as a rapid-fire series of questions flashes by:

- **"What were Todd's pronouns at 2:00 PM on August 14th?"**

- **"Did Jane switch from ve/ver to xe/xir last Wednesday?"**
- **"Which coworker used tree/trees during the Species Affirmation Week?"**

YOUR PALMS SWEAT as you scramble to remember. The timer runs out, and the screen freezes. A final message appears:

"FAILURE: Subject 427 scored 72%. Empathy Band privileges suspended for 72 hours."

YOUR PENALTY? A humiliating demotion to the **Pronoun Probation Program**, where you're required to wear a bright orange badge reading: *"LEARNING IN PROGRESS—PRONOUNS MATTER."*

Scenario 4: The All-Hands Catastrophe

THE STAKES ESCALATE during the company's quarterly All-Hands Meeting, where the entire team gathers in person and online. Every pronoun violation is now broadcast to the entire organization.

MIDWAY through the CEO's speech on *"The Future of Inclusive Accountability,"* you accidentally refer to your boss as **she/her** instead of **ze/zim.** Gasps echo through the room, and the CEO stops mid-sentence.

· · ·

"Subject 427," they say, their tone icy. "Did you just invalidate zim's identity?"

Before you can explain, the InclusiVibe app sends out a company-wide alert:

"Pronoun Violation by Subject 427. Immediate Disciplinary Review Scheduled."

The disciplinary review is a public tribunal, streamed live for maximum humiliation. Your coworkers are invited to provide feedback on how your lack of pronoun awareness has impacted their emotional safety. By the end, your WOKE Score is at zero, and your badge is replaced with one that reads: *"Pronoun Liability: Observe with Caution."*

Escalating Consequences

As your pronoun infractions pile up, the penalties grow increasingly severe:

1. **Social Isolation**: Your desk is relocated to the "Reflection Zone," a glass-walled cubicle where everyone can observe your attempts to reform.
2. **Resource Restriction**: Your access to office supplies is revoked, forcing you to beg coworkers for basic necessities like pens and paper.

3. **Virtual Reality Empathy Training**: A 48-hour immersive simulation where you experience life as a misgendered tweet, bombarded with digital hate until you "learn your lesson."
4. **Public Flogging (Metaphorical)**: A mandatory appearance at the next all-staff meeting, where you're required to deliver a heartfelt apology while reciting the company's Pronoun Creed.

Final Warning: The Pronoun Termination Clause

IF YOUR WOKE Score drops below 50% due to repeated infractions, the company enacts the **Pronoun Termination Clause**. Your employment is terminated with the following statement added to your professional record:

"SUBJECT 427 WAS unable to adapt to the inclusive environment of WOKE WORLD and displayed repeated failures in pronoun respect protocols."

As YOU CLEAN out your desk, your former colleagues watch in silence, their Empathy Bands flashing approving green lights for their compliance.

Closing Note

Pronoun Roulette isn't just a game—it's a high-stakes gauntlet where survival means constant vigilance and perfection. Every interaction is a test, and every mistake brings you closer to the brink of social and professional oblivion. Welcome to WOKE WORLD, where the only way to win is to never, ever lose.

~

Species Identification Day

Welcome to **Species Identification Day**, the one day a week where reality takes a long lunch break and never comes back. Every Friday, employees gather in the Diversity Pavilion—a repurposed conference room now decorated with murals of unicorns, dragons, and abstract blobs labeled "potentially sentient." The air is thick with anticipation, tension, and the faint smell of lavender diffusers because "it calms the inner jaguar."

The Morning Pep Talk

The onboarding leader strides in, their neon blazer casting reflections like a disco ball, clutching a clipboard that screams inclusivity with stickers of dolphins, lions, and... is that a narwhal? They clap their hands, the sound reverberating with manufactured enthusiasm.

"Good morning, everyone! Today's the day we celebrate freedom from the oppressive shackles of speciesism! Remember, humanity is a **social construct**, so feel free to explore the infinite spectrum of existence."

. . .

THE CROWD MURMURS APPROVINGLY. Someone at the back starts a slow clap, but it dies off when the leader's gaze pierces the room.

"TODAY'S AFFIRMATION THEME IS: *'Your Inner Self Is Valid, Even If It's a Ferret.'* So, let's make this a safe, celebratory space for everyone—unless, of course, you identify as human. That's... complicated."

The First Misstep

A BRAVE SOUL in the front row raises their hand, hesitating. "Um, what if I still feel... human?"

THE ROOM FREEZES. The leader's smile tightens, their teeth clenched so hard you'd think they were holding back a scream. "Human?" they repeat, their voice like they've just tasted spoiled milk. "Well, that's... brave. But let's unpack the colonialist undertones of clinging to such a binary identity, shall we?"

A SPOTLIGHT—WHERE did that come from?—shines on the unfortunate questioner. Everyone gasps as the InclusiVibe app sends out an alert:

"SPECIES BIAS DETECTED: Subject 579. Reflection Session Scheduled Immediately."

. . .

THE LEADER SOFTENS THEIR TONE, clearly relishing the opportunity for public correction. "You'll have plenty of time in the Reflection Room to examine why you feel the need to perpetuate anthropocentric dominance. Next question?"

The Declaration Parade

THE HIGHLIGHT of the morning is the **Declaration Parade**, where employees take turns announcing their chosen species. Each declaration is met with cheers, applause, and the occasional tear of solidarity.

A BEAMING ACCOUNTANT STEPS FORWARD. "I identify as a phoenix. My pronouns are flame/flames." The room erupts into applause, someone yells, "Rise from those ashes, queen!"

NEXT IS A NERVOUS INTERN. "Uh... I'm a tree. Pronouns are root/roots." They're met with approving nods, though someone mutters that "trees lack intersectional mobility."

THEN COMES DEREK FROM IT, who strides up confidently. "I'm a velociraptor. My pronouns are rip/tear."

THE LEADER HESITATES, their smile faltering for the first time. "Derek... while we honor your journey, predatory identities can be triggering for herbivore-leaning species. Please reconsider."

· · ·

DEREK SHRUGS AND SITS DOWN, muttering about the systemic erasure of prehistoric voices.

Conflicting Ideologies

THE CHAOS ESCALATES during the **Species Harmony Discussion Circle**, a mandatory event meant to "foster interspecies dialogue." Spoiler: It doesn't.

A LION ROARS THEIR FRUSTRATION. "Why do I have to sit next to a gazelle? This feels like emotional entrapment!"

THE GAZELLE COUNTERS, "As a prey species, your mere presence is violent."

ACROSS THE ROOM, someone identifying as a starfish chimes in. "Can we focus on issues that affect all species, like the systemic exclusion of aquatic voices in land-based conversations?"

THE ROOM DESCENDS INTO CHAOS. A dragon accuses a frog of amphibian privilege. The frog ribbits back that dragons are mythological oppressors. The onboarding leader tries to intervene but is drowned out by a unicorn yelling, "Stop centering hooves in every conversation!"

The Lunchroom Debacle

BY LUNCHTIME, the Species Affirmation Forms are distributed—a 12-page document where you detail your identity, pronouns, and "species-specific dietary accommodations." The cafeteria is divided into sections: carnivores, herbivores, omnivores, and "undefined palates."

YOU CAUTIOUSLY GRAB a tray from the "undefined" line, only to find yourself face-to-face with someone glaring at you.

"YOU'RE EATING TOFU?" they sneer. "Do you know how that impacts sentient plant life?!"

YOU STAMMER AN APOLOGY, but it's too late. The InclusiVibe app buzzes with a notification:

"DIETARY INSENSITIVITY DETECTED. Empathy Score Deduction: -25 Points."

Afternoon Chaos: The Identity Reveal

THE DAY CULMINATES with the **Identity Reveal Ceremony**, where everyone's chosen species is displayed on their digital badges.

YOU NERVOUSLY WATCH as your badge updates:

. . .

SUBJECT 427: Other (Human Leaning).

THE ROOM COLLECTIVELY INHALES, the silence so loud it's deafening. The leader approaches, their face a mask of disappointment.

"OTHER?" they repeat, their voice dripping with disapproval. "Human leaning? Subject 427, do you understand the implications of this choice? By identifying this way, you're perpetuating a harmful binary that invalidates the lived experiences of fluid species."

BEFORE YOU CAN EXPLAIN, your badge flashes again, updating to:

SUBJECT 427: Problematic Pending Review.

THE LEADER SIGHS DRAMATICALLY. "Let's hope next week you choose to unlearn your biases. Dismissed."

The Aftermath

BY THE END of the day, everyone is exhausted. The InclusiVibe app sends out a cheerful wrap-up notification:

"GREAT JOB, team! 87% compliance achieved on Species

Identification Day! Reminder: Next Friday's theme is *'Galactic Identities and Extraterrestrial Pronouns.'* Prepare accordingly."

YOU STAGGER TO YOUR DESK, clutching the Species Self-Affirmation Handbook. Its cover reads: *"Your Journey Beyond Humanity Starts Here."* Inside, Chapter One is titled: "Why Identifying as a Rock Is Revolutionary."

CLOSING Note

Species Identification Day isn't just absurd—it's a psychological endurance test where logic is the only casualty. Every declaration is a battlefield, every conversation a potential minefield, and every choice a ticking time bomb. Welcome to WOKE WORLD, where the only thing more dangerous than being human is admitting it.

The WOKE Starter Pack

CONGRATULATIONS! You've survived onboarding. Your reward? The WOKE Starter Pack, a branded tote bag filled with the essentials for navigating this new world:

1. **Pronoun Badge:** Updates daily. Failure to display it correctly results in immediate termination.
2. **Empathy Manual:** 600 pages of required reading, including chapters like "Why Your Grandmother's Recipes Are a Microaggression" and "The Environmental Impact of Eye Contact."

3. **Species Self-Affirmation Forms:** To be updated monthly. Non-compliance results in a 50% reduction in your WOKE Score.

The onboarding leader hands you the tote with a flourish. "Remember," they whisper, "silence is violence. Speak up—but not too much. That's performative. And smile—but not too wide. That's oppressive."

~

Closing Line: Welcome to the Nightmare

As you stagger out of the onboarding room, clutching your starter pack like a lifeline, your Empathy Band pings with a notification. "Reminder: Your Pronoun Badge updates at midnight. Get it wrong, and you're done."

Welcome to WOKE WORLD. May the odds be ever in your fucking favor.

~

CHAPTER 2

THE NEW RULES OF REALITY — FACTS ARE OPTIONAL, FEELINGS ARE LAW

"Your truth is THE truth, and if it's not, we'll cancel reality itself."

Welcome to the brave new world where facts are about as useful as a flip phone at a tech convention. In WOKE WORLD, reality isn't just flexible—it's optional. Truth isn't what you can prove; it's whatever someone feels it is. And if your reality doesn't align with theirs? Tough shit. Prepare to be canceled harder than a comedian with a problematic tweet from 2007.

THIS IS the New Rules of Reality, where feelings aren't just valid—they're infallible. And if you dare suggest otherwise, congratulations, you're now the newest villain in the never-ending Twitter tribunal.

$\sim$

The Death of Logic: Facts Are So Last Season

ONCE UPON A TIME, people argued with evidence. Now, they argue with emojis. Welcome to the funeral of logic, where facts are deemed "tools of oppression," and questioning someone's feelings is akin to committing war crimes.

SCENARIO: A coworker bursts into a meeting and announces, "The earth is flat."

YOU, being a reasonable human, respond, "Actually, it's a sphere."

BIG MISTAKE.

"ARE YOU INVALIDATING MY LIVED EXPERIENCE?" they hiss, their eyes blazing with righteous fury. The room falls silent as everyone's InclusiVibe app buzzes in unison:

Reality Violation Detected: Subject 427

YOU TRY TO DEFEND YOURSELF. "It's not personal—it's science."

. . .

"SCIENCE?" they shriek, pointing an accusatory finger. "Science is a colonialist construct designed to erase alternative realities!"

BY THE END of the meeting, your WOKE Score has tanked, and HR—sorry, Harmony Regulators—sends you an email:

MANDATORY REALITY SENSITIVITY Training Scheduled

Lived Experience vs. Objective Reality: The War on Evidence

FEELINGS HAVE BECOME the supreme court of truth. It doesn't matter if you have mountains of data, peer-reviewed studies, or photographic evidence. If someone's feelings disagree, they win. End of discussion.

TAKE THE PHENOMENON OF "LIVED EXPERIENCE," a term that started as a way to acknowledge personal perspectives but has now mutated into a weapon to obliterate objective reality.

EXAMPLE: A debate on whether it's raining.

YOU: *It's sunny outside. I can see the clear sky.*

. . .

THEM: *Well, I feel like it's raining, and my lived experience trumps your eyesight.*

SUDDENLY, you're the asshole for daring to trust your senses. By the time the argument's over, they've gathered an online mob accusing you of "weather denialism" and "minimizing the emotional impact of precipitation."

AND DON'T EVEN THINK about asking for evidence. Demanding proof is now considered a microaggression. "Why should I have to justify my truth to you?" they demand, and before you know it, you're blocked, banned, and blacklisted.

~

The New Definition of 'Oppressor': Correcting Someone = Violence

IN WOKE WORLD, providing factual information isn't helpful— it's oppressive. Correcting someone isn't seen as an attempt to clarify or educate; it's rebranded as an act of violence.

SCENARIO: A colleague declares, "The moon landing was fake."

YOU REPLY, "Actually, here's footage, testimonials, and scientific documentation proving it happened."

. . .

WHAT YOU THINK IS a simple correction spirals into a full-blown HR intervention. "Do you understand how invalidating their perspective was?" the Harmony Regulator scolds. "Your obsession with facts reflects a systemic bias against alternative truths."

ALTERNATIVE TRUTHS? **What the actual fuck?**

YOUR PUNISHMENT? A four-hour workshop titled: *"Truth Is a Spectrum: Learning to Respect Alternative Realities."* The presenter, a self-proclaimed "Empathy Alchemist," spends the entire session explaining how "oppressive truth structures" are relics of an outdated, toxic logic system.

~

Public Shaming for Reality-Deniers: When the Mob Comes for You

IN WOKE WORLD, the mob doesn't need pitchforks. They have hashtags. And nothing gets their blood pumping like the scent of a reality-denier.

CASE STUDY: The Great Coffee Cup Catastrophe

YOU'RE at a café and casually mention, "I love how hot this coffee is."

. . .

A STRANGER OVERHEARS. "Hot? That's ableist language! Not everyone experiences temperature the same way."

BEFORE YOU CAN PROCESS the absurdity, they're live-tweeting the interaction. Within hours, #CoffeeGate is trending, your face is plastered across every digital platform, and your inbox is flooded with messages like:

- "How dare you invalidate non-temperature-experiencers?"
- "Hope you choke on your coffee, you bigot."

BY DAY'S END, you're publicly apologizing in a video, holding a sign that says: *I'm sorry for perpetuating the tyranny of thermal privilege.*

Case Study: The Cat Compliment Controversy

YOU'RE SCROLLING through Instagram during your lunch break and come across a photo of a coworker's cat. Harmless, right? Without thinking, you comment, "Such a cute cat!"

BIG MISTAKE.

MOMENTS LATER, your InclusiVibe app buzzes with an alert:

. . .

Objectification Detected: Subject 427. Emotional Safety Violation Logged.

Confused, you check the comments, only to find the original poster replying: "Excuse me? Calling my cat 'cute' reduces it to a superficial aesthetic rather than acknowledging its lived feline experience. This kind of language is harmful and perpetuates pet-owner hierarchies."

Within minutes, #CatGate is trending on all platforms. Your face appears in memes labeled "Pet Oppressor," and you receive a formal notice from HR—sorry, Harmony Regulators:

"Subject 427, your comment has been flagged for objectifying a sentient being. Mandatory attendance at the workshop 'Acknowledging Feline Autonomy: A Journey Toward Linguistic Inclusivity' is required."

The workshop includes a lecture on respecting the emotional complexity of animals, a quiz on non-objectifying adjectives, and a guided meditation to "center the consciousness of companion species." By the end of it, you're required to post a public apology:

"I deeply regret my harmful comment. Cats are more than cute— they are autonomous beings deserving of our full emotional respect."

Escalating Consequences: The Offense of Not Applauding

IT'S the company's weekly Empathy Assembly, where employees are encouraged to celebrate each other's achievements. Todd from IT receives the "Compassionate Emailer of the Week" award for adding heart emojis to his messages. As the room erupts in applause, you hesitate for half a second, distracted by your vibrating Empathy Band.

FATAL ERROR.

YOUR LACK of enthusiasm is flagged by the Harmony Compliance AI, and an announcement blares over the speakers:

"SUBJECT 427 HAS FAILED to meet the required clapping intensity. Emotional Support Level: Substandard. Empathy Score Deduction: -20 Points."

THE ENTIRE ROOM turns to glare at you, their own applause growing louder to compensate for your perceived inadequacy. By the end of the assembly, you're summoned to an emergency Empathy Review Panel, where you're forced to demonstrate proper clapping techniques and write a 500-word essay titled: "Why Everyone Deserves My Full Applause."

～

Escalating Consequences: When Disagreement Becomes a Crime

EVERY TIME you challenge the New Rules of Reality, the consequences get worse:

1 Social Ostracization: Your coworkers stop inviting you to meetings because your "obsession with facts" creates a hostile environment.

2 Digital Blacklisting: The InclusiVibe app flags you as a Reality Denier, locking you out of common areas like the cafeteria or restrooms.

3 Corrective Empathy Training: You're strapped into a VR headset where you experience life as a viral hashtag under relentless public scrutiny.

4 Public Accountability Panels: A tribunal of your peers reviews your infractions, and each one gets live-streamed to the entire organization for maximum humiliation.

Public Accountability Panels: The Theater of Compliance

IMAGINE THIS: you're summoned to a Public Accountability Panel—an Orwellian spectacle masquerading as a team-building exercise. The setting is a brightly lit auditorium, complete with a stage, a podium, and an audience of your coworkers eagerly awaiting the next act of collective humiliation. Overhead, a massive screen flashes the words: *Emotional Transparency: Healing Through Accountability.*

YOUR INFRACTION? During a heated Slack discussion, you dared to suggest that Excel is a superior tool to Google Sheets. A harmless opinion? Think again. The Harmony Compliance AI flagged your comment as "dismissive of alternative software experiences" and escalated it for public review.

The Grand Entrance

As you shuffle onto the stage, clutching the script you've been forced to memorize, the crowd erupts into polite, mandatory applause. The panel—composed of the company's most empathetic employees, handpicked for their high WOKE Scores—sits behind a long table, their faces carefully neutral. At the center is the Head Empathy Alchemist, a self-proclaimed "architect of emotional healing," wearing a rainbow blazer and holding a gavel that glows with LED lights.

"Subject 427," the Alchemist begins, their voice oozing faux compassion. "Today, we are here to address your deeply harmful comment regarding spreadsheet software. Do you understand the gravity of your actions?"

You nod, trying to suppress the urge to roll your eyes. The InclusiVibe app on your wrist vibrates a warning: *Microaggression Detected.*

"Speak up," the Alchemist demands. "Your silence invalidates the emotional labor we've invested in this process."

. . .

"I... I'm sorry," you stammer, reciting the lines drilled into you during your mandatory pre-panel coaching session. "I now realize that my preference for Excel perpetuates a hierarchy of technological privilege, marginalizing those who find Google Sheets more accessible."

The Interrogation

THE PANEL MEMBERS take turns grilling you, each question more ridiculous than the last:

- "How do you plan to make amends to colleagues who felt erased by your pro-Excel stance?"
- "Have you considered the historical context of spreadsheet supremacy and its impact on workplace equity?"
- "What steps will you take to decolonize your approach to data management?"

EVERY RESPONSE you give is met with nods of feigned understanding, though the InclusiVibe alerts on their wrists buzz furiously, measuring the authenticity of your remorse.

The Public Feedback Session

NEXT, the audience is invited to participate. Coworkers step up to the microphone, sharing how your comment personally affected them:

- "When I read the word 'Excel,' I felt a sharp pang of exclusion," says Karen from HR, dabbing at imaginary tears with a tissue. "It reminded me of the time I struggled to learn pivot tables. It was a dark period in my life."
- "I felt triggered," Todd from IT chimes in. "Not everyone has access to Excel at home, and your comment felt like an attack on my socioeconomic status."

THE CROWD MURMURS IN AGREEMENT, their InclusiVibe devices buzzing approvingly.

The Verdict

AFTER AN HOUR of relentless questioning and performative outrage, the panel delivers its decision. The Alchemist slams the glowing gavel, the LED lights pulsing in time with the audience's collective exhale.

"SUBJECT 427, we find you guilty of perpetuating software elitism. Your punishment: a two-week probationary period during which you must exclusively use Google Sheets for all tasks. Additionally, you will attend a three-day workshop titled 'Spreadsheets and Sensitivity: Building a More Inclusive Data Culture.'"

The Aftermath

As you leave the stage, the InclusiVibe app buzzes one last time: *Compliance Achieved. Emotional Transparency Level: Adequate.* The audience applauds—not for you, but for their own participation in this grotesque charade. You're left wondering how much more of your soul you'll have to sacrifice to survive in this dystopian circus.

Final Stage: **Reality Exile**

If your infractions reach critical levels, you're deemed incompatible with WOKE WORLD. You're escorted off the premises while everyone claps—not for you, but for their own compliance.

Escalating Consequences: When Disagreement Becomes a Crime

Every time you challenge the New Rules of Reality, the consequences escalate further into the absurd. But WOKE WORLD isn't content with just punishing you for your present behavior. No, they'll dig into your past—or even your DNA—to ensure compliance spans generations.

Case Study: Apologizing for Ancestral Sins

It's the weekly Inclusivity Checkpoint, a mandatory event where employees gather to "reflect and reconcile" any biases lurking in their subconscious. Just as you think you've survived the worst of it, the Harmony Regulator announces the newest company-wide initiative: **Ancestral Bias Accountability.**

. . .

"WITH ADVANCEMENTS IN DNA ANALYSIS," the Regulator chirps, holding up a sleek tablet, "we can now identify the biases embedded in your ancestral lineage. This breakthrough allows us to hold you accountable not just for your own behaviors but for the prejudices of your forebears. After all, silence on generational sins is still violence."

THE ROOM IS SILENT, save for the sound of collective bewilderment. Then your InclusiVibe app buzzes:

"SUBJECT 427: New Task Assigned. Apologize for Ancestral Bias Detected via DNA Analysis."

CURIOUS—AND horrified—you open the task details to find the following summary:

"DNA ANALYSIS REVEALS that your great-great-grandfather participated in environmentally destructive farming practices. This legacy has contributed to systemic ecological harm. Immediate action required: Record a public apology acknowledging the harm caused by your ancestor and detailing steps you're taking to atone."

BEFORE YOU CAN PROCESS the absurdity, your badge updates:

SUBJECT 427: Ancestral Bias Pending Reconciliation.

· · ·

You're then informed that failure to comply will result in a WOKE Score deduction and mandatory attendance at the upcoming workshop: "Healing the Past: Owning the Sins of Your Ancestors." The seminar includes:

- A guided meditation to connect with your "inner ancestor."
- A worksheet titled "How Would Your Forebears Respond to Modern Inclusivity Standards?"
- A public speaking segment where you confess your ancestor's sins while holding a ceremonial DNA scroll.

As you stand in front of your colleagues, apologizing for a man you never met who used too much fertilizer in 1892, you realize logic isn't just dead. It's been cremated, buried, and replaced with a hologram of feelings.

~

The Death of Debate: Silence or Surrender

WOKE WORLD doesn't allow dissent. There's no middle ground, no gray area. You either agree wholeheartedly, or you're the enemy.

Gone are the days of healthy debates. Now, every conversation is a landmine, every disagreement a declaration of war. You're not just wrong—you're dangerous.

~

Closing Line: The New Reality

Logic is dead. Empathy reigns supreme. Feel it. Fake it. Or be fucking erased. Welcome to the New Rules of Reality, where facts are optional, feelings are law, and compliance is survival. But remember: in WOKE WORLD, even silence is violence.

CHAPTER 3

PRONOUN WARS — MAY THE BEST PRONOUN WIN

"It's not just grammar anymore. It's war."

~

Language wasn't supposed to be a battlefield, but now? It's a damn bloodsport. Words aren't for communication anymore—they're loaded fucking guns, and pronouns are the hollow-point bullets waiting to rip through your existence. Welcome to the *Pronoun Wars,* where survival doesn't mean being right; it means *shutting the hell up and hoping nobody notices you breathing wrong.*

THIS ISN'T CONVERSATION. It's *combat.* Every syllable is a tripwire, every sentence a sniper in the bushes, and every damn pronoun is a tactical nuke. Get one wrong, and BOOM—you're obliterated. No trial. No mercy. Just your career, your reputation, and your entire life reduced to ash in the fiery explosion of mob outrage.

. . .

PRONOUNS AREN'T about identity anymore. They're *weapons of mass destruction.* The moment you step into a conversation, you're already in the kill zone. Say the wrong word, and the *Pronoun Police* won't just correct you—they'll fucking *gut you* in the public square.

ACCIDENTALLY MISGENDER SOMEONE? Doesn't matter if it's 2 AM and you haven't slept in three days. *Intent doesn't matter.* Mistakes don't matter. All that matters is that you stepped on the social landmine, and now you're bleeding out on the battlefield of *progress.*

THIS ISN'T GRAMMAR; this is *fucking war.* It's not about connecting with people. It's about *not getting executed.* There's no room for error, no forgiveness, and sure as hell, no second chances. One wrong step, and you're plastered all over Twitter with hashtags like #PronounBigot or #LinguisticTerrorist.

SO WELCOME TO the *Pronoun Wars.* Don't bother bringing logic or context—they're as useless as a helmet in a nuclear blast. Here, survival means saying nothing, doing nothing, and praying to whatever gods still give a shit that nobody calls on you to speak. Because in this game, even silence can be weaponized. And when the mob comes for you? *They don't just want an apology—they want your head on a fucking spike.*

~

Pronoun Roulette: Spin the Wheel of Doom

At WOKE WORLD, your pronouns aren't just a part of your identity—they're a part of *your job description*. Every morning at 9:00 AM sharp, the InclusiVibe app pings with your daily pronoun update. Forget your coffee; the first thing you need to do is check whether you're a "ze/zir," "fae/faer," or something experimental like "cloud/clouds."

Scenario: The Morning Misstep

It's Monday morning, and you're already running late. You grab your phone and see the dreaded notification:

"Good morning! Today, your pronouns are xe/xem. Remember: Failure to respect pronouns can result in disciplinary action. Have a great day!"

You groan but make a mental note. Unfortunately, mental notes don't survive the morning rush. By the time you get to work, you've already forgotten.

At the water cooler, you run into Chloe from Marketing—whose pronouns were "she/her" yesterday. Still groggy, you ask, "Hey, did *she* finish the budget report?"

Chloe freezes. The room goes silent. Your Empathy Band vibrates violently, alerting everyone within a 10-foot radius of your heinous crime. The InclusiVibe app blares a notification:

. . .

"Pronoun Violation Detected: Subject 427. Empathy Score Deduction: -15 Points."

Chloe glares at you, tears welling up in her eyes. "Excuse me, *xem*! Did you just misgender me? Do you have any idea how invalidating that is?"

Before you can stammer out an apology, a Pronoun Compliance Officer materializes from the HR void, clipboard in hand. "Subject 427, please follow me," they say, their tone dripping with condescension.

~

The Cost of Misgendering: Pay Up or Shut Up

Misgendering isn't just a social faux pas anymore—it's a corporate crime. The first offense might earn you a stern talking-to but don't get too comfortable. Repeat offenders face escalating consequences that make traffic tickets look like Monopoly money.

Fines for Feelings

Accidentally refer to someone as "he" instead of "they"? That'll cost you $50, automatically deducted from your paycheck. Forget someone's neo-pronouns? Congrats, you've just earned a $100 fine. And if you dare to argue? You're looking at mandatory "Empathy

Re-education Training" and a public apology posted on the company Slack.

Case Study: The Bathroom Blunder

THE OFFICE BATHROOM used to be a sanctuary, a place where you could hide from awkward conversations. Not anymore. At WOKE WORLD, every bathroom stall has a digital pronoun display, updated daily to reflect the identities of its users.

YOU'RE in a rush and accidentally step into the stall designated for "cloud/clouds." A colleague catches you in the act.

"ARE YOU SERIOUS?" they gasp. "Did you even *check* the stall display? Do you know how invalidating this is for clouds everywhere?"

YOUR EMPATHY BAND BUZZES FURIOUSLY. Within minutes, the incident is reported, and you receive a Slack message from Harmony Regulators:

"SUBJECT 427, your unauthorized use of the 'cloud/clouds' stall has been flagged. Please complete the 'Respecting Spatial Pronouns' training by the end of the day."

Rise of the Pronoun Police: Big Brother Has Pronouns

IF YOU THOUGHT your coworkers were bad, wait until you meet the Pronoun Compliance Officers. These self-righteous grammar enforcers patrol the office like linguistic bounty hunters armed with clipboards, digital scanners, and a God complex.

Scenario: The Team Meeting Interrogation

IT'S WEDNESDAY, and you're sitting in a team meeting. The topic? Quarterly sales projections. But before anyone can discuss numbers, a Pronoun Compliance Officer interrupts.

"BEFORE WE PROCEED, let's go around the room and share our pronouns," they announce. "And remember, if you fail to update your daily pronouns, you'll be flagged for non-compliance."

EVERYONE OBEDIENTLY RECITES THEIR IDENTITIES:

- **"Xe/xem."**
- **"Fae/faer."**
- **"Star/stars."**

WHEN IT'S YOUR TURN, you freeze. You forgot to check the app this morning.

THE COMPLIANCE OFFICER narrows their eyes. "Subject 427, you seem... hesitant. Do you not know your own pronouns?"

. . .

Your Empathy Band vibrates like a ticking time bomb. The room stares, waiting for you to fumble. You blurt out, "Uh, cloud/clouds?"

The Compliance Officer smirks, clearly unimpressed. "Nice try, but clouds were *yesterday*. Your actual pronouns are fae/faer. Please report to HR for corrective action."

The Empathy Re-education Gauntlet

For those who repeatedly fumble their way through the *Pronoun Wars,* there's no escaping the grim fate that awaits: **The Empathy Re-Education Gauntlet.** This three-day Orwellian nightmare, designed to "reprogram your biases," is less of a workshop and more of a psychological boot camp aimed at annihilating any remaining shred of independent thought.

Day 1: Pronoun Immersion Therapy — Becoming the Victim

The Gauntlet begins with **Pronoun Immersion Therapy,** a baptism of fire that plunges participants into the lived experience of pronouns themselves. Each person is strapped into a VR headset loaded with *Pronoun Simulator 3000,* a sadistic program that forces you to navigate life as "they/them," "xe/xem," or some other linguistic aberration of the day.

. . .

YOU STROLL through a virtual workplace where everyone aggressively misgenders you. "Excuse me, *sir*—I mean *ma'am*—I mean... whatever the fuck you are!" The headset buzzes every time you're misgendered, delivering sharp jolts of discomfort to the sides of your head. By the time the program finishes, your temples are throbbing, and your self-respect has been ground into dust.

THE SIMULATION DOESN'T STOP at simple misgendering. It ramps up with scenes where coworkers roll their eyes when you correct them, or HR assigns you a public "They Awareness Day." The session ends with a virtual mob chasing you, chanting, "Respect our pronouns or die!" You're left sweating, disoriented, and teetering on the edge of a breakdown.

Day 2: Public Apology Bootcamp — Grovel Like You Mean It

NO ONE LEAVES Day 2 with their dignity intact. Here, participants are subjected to **Public Apology Bootcamp,** a brutal session designed to perfect the art of corporate groveling.

YOU'RE HANDED a script that bans weak-ass phrases like, *"I'm sorry if you were offended"* or *"That wasn't my intention."* Instead, you're required to say,

"I DEEPLY REGRET my oppressive behavior. My actions contributed to the erasure of marginalized identities, and I will strive every day to unlearn my harmful biases."

· · ·

BUT APOLOGIZING ISN'T ENOUGH—YOU must *perform* your apology. HR coaches you on the appropriate amount of eye contact, vocal tremor, and tears to convey "genuine remorse." Can't summon tears on demand? No problem—they'll spritz you with saline solution to simulate weeping.

ONCE PERFECTED, your apology is **live-streamed to the company Slack channel.** Employees are encouraged to leave feedback ranging from,

- *"This felt authentic—good job!"*

to

- *"Lacked emotional vulnerability. Try harder."*

ANY CRITICISM SENDS you back for another round of coaching, ensuring you don't leave until you can grovel like a pro.

Day 3: The Pronoun Gauntlet — The Final Humiliation

THE LAST DAY of the Gauntlet is the most sadistic: **The Pronoun Gauntlet.** This high-stakes final exam requires participants to identify 100 different pronouns in under 60 seconds. Fail, and you're sent straight back to Day 1.

. . .

THE TEST BEGINS WITH "BASIC" pronouns like *"he/him"* and *"she/her,"* lulling you into a false sense of security. But by the time you hit pronoun #20, the list veers into uncharted territory with monstrosities like *"star/stars,"* *"e/eirs,"* and *"zho/zhir."*

AS THE CLOCK TICKS DOWN, the questions grow increasingly absurd:

- *"What are Alex's pronouns during the fall equinox?"*
- *"How does Jamie's pronoun set change after 5 PM on Fridays?"*
- *"Which coworker identifies as 'void/voidself' during team-building activities?"*

STUMBLE, stammer, or hesitate for even a millisecond, and the buzzer sounds, blasting **"BIGOT ALERT"** through the room. The failure is broadcast live to your coworkers, who gleefully spam Slack with "🙄" and "🚫" emojis to signal their disapproval.

TO PASS, you not only have to get every answer right but do so with *enthusiasm.* The judges, a panel of *Pronoun Compliance Officers* with WOKE Scores so high they practically glow, scrutinize your every move. "Did you hesitate before saying *zho/zhir?* That's a microaggression," they bark, docking points.

The Aftermath

IF, by some miracle, you survive all three days, you're handed a certificate that reads:

"THIS IS to certify that [Your Name] has successfully completed Empathy Re-Education Training and is now an ally of inclusive excellence."

BUT DON'T THINK the nightmare ends there. Failure to *display* your newfound empathy at all times means HR can revoke your certificate at any moment, throwing you right back into the Gauntlet.

The Return to the Workplace

WHEN YOU REJOIN YOUR TEAM, it's obvious you've been through hell. Your eyes are hollow, your confidence shattered, and your Inclusi-Vibe app is now programmed to send hourly reminders:

- *"Respect pronouns."*
- *"Silence is violence."*
- *"Grovel harder."*

COWORKERS EITHER AVOID eye contact or offer patronizing smiles, knowing full well that you've been broken. And if you thought surviving the Gauntlet earned you respect, think again. "Did you *really* learn anything," Karen from HR whispers loudly during lunch. "Or are you just faking it?"

Welcome to Re-education Hell

THE EMPATHY RE-EDUCATION Gauntlet isn't just training—it's a damn *purge*. It strips you of individuality, crushes your will, and molds you into a compliant drone who reflexively genuflects at the altar of pronouns.

BY THE END, you're not just a survivor of the Pronoun Wars. You're a fucking *casualty*. Welcome to the Gauntlet, where the only way out is complete and total surrender—or an early retirement filled with PTSD flashbacks of *"xe/xem"* and *"quantum/quantums."*

The Pronoun Hunger Games

AT THE APEX of the *Pronoun Wars* lies the pinnacle of corporate lunacy: **The Pronoun Hunger Games.** Imagine *The Hunger Games* crossed with a woke HR seminar sprinkled with the sadistic glee of a Roman coliseum. This annual bloodbath pits employees against each other in a soul-crushing competition to prove their undying devotion to the *Cult of Pronouns*.

The Rules

1. Memorize the Madness

EVERY PARTICIPANT IS HANDED a *Pronoun Bible*—a 500-page document detailing the personal pronouns of every employee, contractor, and damn intern. From the straightforward (he/him, she/her) to the surreal (quantum/quantums, void/voidself), nothing is off the table. And yes, you're expected to remember them all. *Every single one.*

2. **Rapid-Fire Rounds**

IN EACH ROUND, participants face the *Pronoun Gauntlet,* a ruthless interrogation where judges bark out questions like,

- *"What are Todd from IT's pronouns at 3 PM on Thursdays during Leap Years?"*
- *"How does Marcia from Marketing's pronoun set shift during a waxing gibbous moon?"*

STUMBLE? Stammer? Blink too fucking slowly? Congratulations, you're out. Your name is projected on the *Wall of Shame* alongside a message:

"SUBJECT 427 FAILED TO HONOR PRONOUN DIVERSITY. Empathy Score: ZERO."

3. **No Mercy**

THERE ARE NO LIFELINES, no retries, and sure as hell, no grace for the sleep-deprived or emotionally drained. One wrong answer, and you're booted out faster than a problematic tweet in 2023.

The Carnage

THE GAMES ARE a spectacle of suffering. Employees stumble over words like *"zoi/zoir"* and *"interdimensional/quantumself,"* sweating under the cold gaze of the *Pronoun Police* as they fumble with flash-cards and desperately scroll through their InclusiVibe app.

Picture this:

TODD FROM IT, drenched in sweat, stammers as he tries to remember whether Susan from HR shifts from *xe/xem* to *fae/faer* after her third kombucha. The audience gasps as the buzzer sounds. Todd's out. The *Empathy Enforcer* steps forward, slapping a red sticker on his chest:

"PRONOUN FAIL: BIASED AGAINST FAER FOLK."

THE JUDGES DON'T JUST ELIMINATE you—they eviscerate you. "How *dare* you erase Marcia's unique lunar pronouns? Do you understand the emotional labor it takes for her to maintain her waxing-gibbous identity?!" Todd hangs his head in shame as the audience boos him into oblivion.

The Winner

ONE PERSON—*AND only one*—emerges victorious. The **Pronoun Champion.** Their reward? The coveted Pronoun Immunity Badge, a glowing lanyard that spares them from fines, workshops, and the constant terror of misgendering for an entire year.

. . .

THE REST? Back to the *linguistic trenches,* where every interaction is a potential minefield and every pronoun a death trap.

Why It Exists

WHY DOES the *Pronoun Hunger Games* exist? Officially, it's to "promote inclusive excellence." Unofficially, it's because HR loves watching people squirm. It's a sadistic HR-wet dream wrapped in a rainbow bow, giving management an excuse to enforce compliance through public humiliation while claiming to celebrate diversity.

The Aftermath

THE LOSERS LEAVE the arena broken and battered, their InclusiVibe apps buzzing with penalties:

- *"Pronoun Sensitivity Training Scheduled."*
- *"Mandatory Public Apology: Why I Failed the LGBTQIA2+ Pronoun Gauntlet."*
- *"Empathy Score Deduction: -30."*

THE WINNERS? They spend the next year lording their immunity over their coworkers like pronoun royalty, safe in the knowledge that, for once, they can speak without fear of instant cancellation.

Closing Note

THE *PRONOUN HUNGER Games* isn't just a contest—it's a fucking *crucible.* It's where careers are destroyed, dignity is annihilated, and linguistic compliance is elevated to an art form. Welcome to the *Pronoun Wars.* Spin wisely, speak carefully, and for the love of whatever deity you still believe in, *don't you dare fuck it up.*

~

Closing Line: Welcome to Pronoun Roulette

PRONOUNS AREN'T JUST GRAMMAR ANYMORE—THEY'RE warfare. One wrong word, one slip of the tongue, and you're toast. Welcome to Pronoun Roulette. Spin wisely, or you're fired.

~

CHAPTER 4

PARENTAL ANARCHY — RAISING WOLVES, FROGS, AND STATE-OWNED CHILDREN

"My child identifies as a pterodactyl. You'd better affirm it."

Once upon a time, parenting was simple: keep your kids alive, teach them not to be assholes, and maybe—just maybe—prepare them for adulthood. But welcome to WOKE WORLD, where parenting isn't about raising functional humans anymore. It's about affirming your child's every whim, no matter how unhinged. Your kid wants to identify as a velociraptor? You'd better be ready to learn dino-pronouns and build a Jurassic habitat in the backyard—or face a SWAT team of Child Protective Services officers armed with rainbow tasers.

PARENTING HAS OFFICIALLY GONE FERAL. Schools are zoos, your house is a species sanctuary, and the state has more custody over your kid than you do. Buckle up because, in WOKE WORLD, you're not a parent. You're a compliance officer in a biological shitstorm.

~

Species-Affirming Schools: Frogs, Dragons, and Pterodactyls, Oh My!

THE FIRST DAY of school used to be about backpacks and peanut-free lunches. Now, it's about filling out a **Species Affirmation Form**. You're handed a clipboard by a teacher who looks like they just got back from Burning Man, complete with glitter eyebrows and a nose ring shaped like a peace sign.

"Please declare your child's species," they chirp. "This is a safe space for all identities, whether they hop, roar, or fly."

YOU HESITATE, glancing at your kid. Yesterday, they were obsessed with dinosaurs. Today, they've decided they're a frog. You clear your throat. "Uh, amphibian?"

THE TEACHER BEAMS. "Ribbit-affirming—love that for them! We'll make sure their experience is fully frogtastic." They scribble something on a clipboard and slap a sticker on your kid's chest that says, *"Hoppy to Be Me!"*

. . .

By mid-morning, your child is knee-deep in the **Species Immersion Curriculum**. While you were hoping they'd learn multiplication, they're busy croaking in unison with their classmates during "Frog Affirmation Hour." Instead of math class, there's "Pond Safety 101." Science class? Forget about it. It's now "Bug-Eating Best Practices."

And don't even think about questioning the curriculum. A parent at the last PTA meeting dared to suggest that the whole *"Frogs Are Valid"* initiative was distracting from core academics. The school immediately issued a **Species Bias Alert**, and by the next morning, their lawn was covered in picket signs that read, *"Support Amphibians or Die Trying!"*

Schools are zoos, kids are barking at teachers, and the Re-Gender Party has turned classrooms into a circus of identity chaos. But who let this insanity in through the front door? The parents. That's who.

~

The Parents: Enablers of Chaos

Let's not sugarcoat it—the kids in the Pronoun Wars, the Species Affirmation Zoo, and the Re-Gender Circus didn't get there on their own. Behind every frog-identified child, dragon-obsessed kindergartener, and wolf-howling tween is a parent who's so deep in the WOKE Kool-Aid they're practically drowning in it. These parents aren't just clueless—they're complicit. They've traded common sense for likes on Instagram and swapped parental authority for woke performance art.

. . .

Meet the Fucked-Up Parents

1. The Instagram Martyr:

THESE PARENTS DON'T CARE about their kids' "identity" as much as they care about broadcasting it to the world. They're the ones posting tearful videos on TikTok about their child's "journey" to discovering they're a phoenix, complete with dramatic piano music and hashtags like #ProudPhoenixParent and #WingsOfLove.

THE KID COULD BE SITTING in the corner gnawing on a stuffed unicorn, but Mom's too busy editing her next viral post to notice. When someone dares to comment, *"Hey, maybe your kid doesn't need a $5,000 custom phoenix costume,"* she responds with a 12-paragraph rant about "oppression," "species erasure," and how *"parents like me are doing the hard work of creating a better world."*

SPOILER ALERT: That kid grows up with a therapy bill longer than the fucking Dead Sea Scrolls.

2. The Overcompensating Dad:

THIS IS the guy who spent his entire childhood being bullied for wearing Velcro shoes and now thinks the only way to redeem himself is by being the "coolest, most accepting dad on the planet."

. . .

His 6-year-old comes home and says, "I'm a velociraptor," and instead of saying, *"No, you're not. Eat your chicken nuggets,"* this clown is at the hardware store building a DIY dinosaur enclosure in the backyard.

At school pickup, he's the one wearing a Jurassic Park T-shirt and explaining to other parents how *"raptor culture has been historically marginalized."* When his kid inevitably declares a new identity as a space alien, Dad's out there spray-painting a UFO on the minivan and learning Klingon just to stay relevant.

This isn't parenting. It's cosplay with child-sized consequences.

3. The Competition Queen:

This mom isn't just along for the ride—she's here to *win*. If Karen down the street is raising a wolf, you can bet your ass this one's kid is a *direwolf*.

> **"Oh, your kid's a dragon?" she sneers. "How cute. My daughter's a multiverse dragon—she exists in 14 dimensions simultaneously."**

When the school announces a "Species Spirit Day," this lunatic hires a Hollywood special effects team to create a smoke-breathing dragon costume for her child. If another parent tries to one-up her, she'll go nuclear, calling CPS on them for "species neglect."

THE KID, meanwhile, is visibly exhausted, begging for mac and cheese while Mom shoves kale chips down their throat because *"dragons are vegan, sweetheart."*

4. The Trauma Tourist:

THEN THERE'S the parent who treats their child's identity crisis as their own personal pity party. Every PTA meeting, every parent-teacher conference, every damn soccer game, they're there, talking about how *"hard"* it is to have a kid who identifies as a unicorn.

"DO you know how much emotional labor goes into supporting a unicorn child?" they'll sob, wiping fake tears with a monogrammed handkerchief. "I've spent hours finding the right glitter for their horn!"

THEY DON'T ACTUALLY GIVE a shit about their kid's happiness. They just want to be the center of attention, reveling in the sympathy of other parents while their child sits in the corner, wondering why their horn looks like a discarded pool noodle.

5. The DIY Lunatic:

Meet the parent who takes "support" to a deranged new level. Their child identifies as a monkey? This lunatic isn't just buying a banana costume—they're converting the entire backyard into a damn rainforest. We're talking vines, jungle gyms, and imported tropical plants, complete with a misting system to replicate "authentic monkey humidity."

But wait, it gets better. The week after this $15,000 renovation is complete, their kid announces, "I'm actually a snake now!" So, what does this lunatic do? Rips out the jungle installs heat lamps, and orders a 50-pound bag of frozen mice for feeding time. Meanwhile, their neighbors are staring out the window, wondering if they should call the HOA or Animal Control.

6. **The Corporate Sellout:**

Then there's the parent who sees dollar signs instead of boundaries. Their kid declares themselves a unicorn, and within a week, they've launched a line of species-themed merch: "Sparkle Horn" backpacks, "Magic Mane" hair dye, and glitter-filled "Unicorn Tears" water bottles.

Not content with just merch, these parents go all-in on monetizing their child's identity. They start a YouTube channel called *"Daily Life of a Unicorn,"* where their kid prances around the house in pastel costumes, eating organic oats out of a golden bowl. Millions of subscribers later, the child is exhausted, the parents are raking in sponsorship deals, and the dog is wearing a rainbow tail because "family branding is key."

. . .

The Fallout of Parental Madness

THESE PARENTS AREN'T RAISING **children. They're raising confused, overindulged narcissists who think the world revolves around their every whim.** By refusing to set boundaries, these enablers create a generation of kids who believe feelings are facts, biology is optional, and reality bends to their desires.

WHEN THESE KIDS hit adulthood and realize the world doesn't give a single shit about their "species identity," guess who they'll blame? Not themselves. Not the system. Nope—they'll turn right back to Mommy and Daddy, asking why the hell they let them grow up thinking they were a pterodactyl.

THE ANSWER? **Because these parents weren't strong enough to say, "No, you're not a wolf. You're a child, and it's bedtime." Instead, they chose the path of least resistance, sacrificing their kids' futures at the altar of woke validation.**

Closing Note: The Real Villains

BEHIND EVERY "SPECIES-AFFIRMING" classroom and CPS intervention is a parent who handed over the leash—or reins, or damn wings. These aren't heroes. They're cowards, sellouts, and clowns in a circus they helped build. So the next time you see a kid at the park barking at pigeons, don't blame the child. Blame the fucking moron who handed them a wolf collar and called it love.

~

The Re-Gender Party: A Quarterly Clusterfuck

EVERY QUARTER, the school hosts a **Re-Gender and Species Party**, a mandatory celebration where children are encouraged to "shed their old selves" and embrace their "new truth." Picture a cross between a Pride parade, a furry convention, and a medieval coronation. That's your child's third-grade classroom now.

AT THE EVENT, children are led onto a stage one by one, where they announce their new species, gender, and name for the semester. Teachers, parents, and classmates cheer wildly, no matter how absurd the declaration.

"TODAY, I'M NOT MAX ANYMORE," your kid announces. "I'm Fang the Fearless Wolf! My pronouns are howl/howls!"

THE CROWD GOES WILD. Teachers throw confetti. The principal shouts into a megaphone, "HOWL FOR HOWL!"

AS YOU SIT THERE CLAPPING, you can't help but wonder when your life turned into a damn circus. But you'd better keep smiling. The parent sitting next to you once laughed during a "Lizard Affirmation" ceremony. CPS showed up at their house the next day, accusing them of "emotional violence against reptiles."

State Seizes Your Children: CPS Wants Your Kid More Than You Do

THINK you're still in charge of your kid? Think again. The state owns them now, and they're not shy about flexing that power. In WOKE WORLD, refusing to affirm your child's identity—no matter how insane—is treated like abuse. Don't believe me? Ask Karen from down the street.

KAREN'S 7-YEAR-OLD decided they were a phoenix, complete with fiery wings and an immortal soul. Karen, a single mom who works two jobs, made the critical mistake of telling her kid, "Honey, you're not a phoenix. You're a human child."

THE NEXT DAY, the school counselor filed a report with CPS. By the end of the week, Karen's kid was in foster care, living with a couple who owned a pet parrot and called themselves "Avian Allies." Karen, meanwhile, was court-ordered to attend a **Species Sensitivity Bootcamp** and write a 2,000-word essay titled *"Why I Will Never Erase My Child's Inner Phoenix Again."*

~

Compliance Isn't Optional

NONCOMPLIANCE ISN'T JUST FROWNED upon—it's illegal. If you don't affirm your child's species, the consequences are swift and brutal. Fines, mandatory workshops, public shaming—it's all on the table. And the state doesn't stop at taking your kids; they'll take your dignity, too.

. . .

Case Study: The Crocodile Chronicles

LAST YEAR, a dad in Florida refused to buy his 5-year-old a custom crocodile tail for Halloween. He argued that his kid would grow out of their "crocodile phase." Big mistake. The school filed a **Species Neglect Report**, and the dad was hauled into court.

THE JUDGE DIDN'T MINCE words. "By refusing to affirm your child's crocodilian identity, you have inflicted severe emotional trauma," he declared. The dad was sentenced to six months of mandatory Species Affirmation Counseling and ordered to purchase a deluxe crocodile costume for his child, complete with animatronic jaws.

~

The Cost of Species Affirmation

IT'S NOT JUST your sanity on the line—it's your wallet, too. Species affirmation isn't cheap, and schools aren't shy about passing the costs onto parents.

FIELD TRIPS NOW INVOLVE TRANSPORTING children to "habitat-appropriate" locations. If your kid identifies as a shark, you're footing the bill for their class trip to the nearest aquarium. If they're a dragon, expect to pay for a private tour of a castle. One mom had to refinance her house to afford her kid's **"Pond Relocation Experience"**—a weekend retreat for frog-identified children to "reconnect with their amphibious roots."

. . .

AND DON'T EVEN GET me started on the **Species Supply List**. Gone are the days of crayons and notebooks. Now, you're buying insect nets for frog kids, chew toys for wolf kids, and fireproof blankets for phoenix kids. One dad in Ohio went bankrupt after his daughter declared herself a unicorn and demanded a solid gold horn.

~

The Parent Shaming Olympics

THINK you can fake it 'til you make it? Think again. In WOKE WORLD, it's not enough to comply—you have to *perform* your compliance. Every species-affirming parent is in a constant competition to prove they're more woke than the next.

EXAMPLE: At last year's school fundraiser, a mom showed up dressed as a velociraptor to support her "raptor-identified" child. Not to be outdone, another parent arrived in a full-scale dragon costume, complete with smoke effects. By the end of the night, one dad had hired a falconry expert to give a live demonstration in honor of his "hawk-identified" son.

THE EVENT ENDED with a literal pissing contest—one wolf-identified dad peed on a tree to prove his allegiance to the pack. He won a trophy for "Most Dedicated Parent."

~

Closing Line: The New Normal

YOUR KID'S A WOLF. Your neighbor's a dragon. And if you're not howling at the moon by nightfall, CPS will drag you out of your house, leash you up, and toss you in the nearest kennel. Welcome to WOKE WORLD, where parenting is optional, but compliance is mandatory—and noncompliance isn't just punished, it's fucking annihilated.

CHAPTER 5

PLAYING GOD WITH GENDER: THE PARENTAL DELUSION OF REDESIGNING REALITY

"When your kid is deciding between peanut butter or jelly, maybe don't let them pick their gender."

~

To eviscerate the trend of parents making life-altering gender decisions for children who can't even tie their shoes yet and to skewer the insanity of giving 10-year-olds the reins to their biological destiny. This chapter should be unapologetically raw, hyper-critical, and designed to leave no room for ambiguity in its stance.

~

The Introduction: Welcome to the Gender Lab

ONCE UPON A TIME, parents taught their kids how to read, write, and not shit their pants in public. But in WOKE WORLD, parenting means playing Frankenstein with your kid's gender.

YOUR TODDLER PREFERS the pink blanket over the blue one? Boom—clearly, they're transgender, and you'd better call the doctor to schedule hormone blockers before lunchtime. Your 10-year-old thinks it might be "fun" to try being a girl. Awesome—let's order puberty blockers on Amazon Prime and start shopping for bras.

THIS ISN'T PARENTING. It's biological malpractice disguised as progress, and the casualties are the kids stuck in the middle of their parents' woke performance art. The reality is, when it comes to gender, these parents are so hell-bent on being progressive that they've gone fully regressive—turning children into guinea pigs in an experiment that no one asked for.

∼

The Trend of Parental "Gender Deciders"

"When Your Kid Can't Spell Their Name, Maybe Don't Rewrite Their Gender."

MEET THE "GENDER DECIDERS," parents so drunk on woke Kool-Aid that they think their 3-year-old's favorite toy truck is a definitive sign of manhood—or lack thereof. Forget potty training; these geniuses are busy booking gender consultations with pediatric endocrinologists because little Timmy picked a Barbie doll instead of a G.I. Joe.

Case Study: The Birthday Disaster

Take Heather and Dave—parents who decided their toddler wasn't "expressing their true gender." At their kid's *third* birthday party, instead of cake and balloons, they handed out "gender reveal" cupcakes. The kid just wanted chocolate. Instead, they were forced to sit through a ceremony where Mommy and Daddy declared, "From now on, Emma is Evan! He's a big boy now!"

The result? A confused child who spends their afternoons eating crayons while Heather posts Instagram stories about "breaking the binary." Meanwhile, Evan doesn't know his colors yet, but sure, let's bet the farm he knows his gender identity.

~

The DIY Gender Architects: When Parents Hand Over the Keys to the Kids

"Oh, You're 10 and Want to Be a Girl? Sounds Great! Let's Block Your Puberty!"

The other side of this circus is parents who let their kids make monumental life decisions before they can even legally use TikTok. These are the parents who think it's "empowering" to let a 10-year-old declare, "I'm a girl now," while ignoring the long-term consequences.

Puberty Blocker Playdates

THE NEW STATUS symbol for these woke warriors? Being the first parent on the block to put their kid on hormone blockers. Forget swimming lessons or piano practice. It's all about documenting their child's "brave journey" through gender transition on social media, complete with hashtags like #TransKidsAreMagic and #HormonesForHappiness.

AND IF ANYONE dares to ask, "Hey, isn't this kind of a huge decision for someone who still believes in Santa?" they're immediately labeled transphobic and banned from every PTA meeting in town.

The Gender Wizard Hotline

"Dial-a-Gender: The Gender Wizard Hotline"

FOR PARENTS DROWNING in the overwhelming responsibility of letting their toddlers "discover their true selves," WOKE WORLD offers a groundbreaking solution: the Gender Wizard Hotline. Just dial 1-800-GENDR-WIZ and get instant clarity on your child's identity—for the low price of $29.99 per minute.

THE SERVICE FEATURES A TEAM OF "CERTIFIED" Gender Gurus with advanced degrees in Wokeology and TikTok Studies, standing by 24/7 to help parents navigate their child's complex identity journey. Whether you're dealing with a preschooler who insists they're a nonbinary snow leopard or a middle-schooler questioning whether they're "quantum-gender," the Gender Wizard Hotline is here to provide definitive answers.

Sample Call Transcript:

PARENT: "Hi, my 4-year-old says they're a dragon but also likes princess dresses. What do I do?"

GENDER GURU: "Congratulations! Your child is clearly a Dragon-Paladin Demi-Princess. I suggest starting them on a diet of glitter-infused kale chips to honor their dual identities. Also, book a therapy session to process the societal pressures they'll face in embracing this truth."

FOR AN EXTRA $50, you can even get a custom pronoun set emailed directly to your child's daycare, ensuring compliance across all staff and peers. Remember: if you hesitate to use the hotline, you're risking emotional violence against your child. Don't wait—consult the Wizard today!

The Science Parents Love to Ignore

"Facts? We Don't Need No Stinking Facts!"

ASK any of these parents about the irreversible effects of hormone blockers or the mental health risks associated with rushing a child into gender transition, and they'll call you a "science denier." The irony? The very studies they wave around to justify their decisions often warn against making these choices prematurely.

- **Puberty Blockers:** Often hailed as "reversible," the reality is far murkier. Studies show these medications can stunt growth, affect brain development, and lead to lifelong infertility.
- **Surgical Interventions:** Some parents are greenlighting irreversible surgeries for teenagers who haven't even finished high school. We're talking double mastectomies for 14-year-olds because they *might* identify as male.

THESE PARENTS AREN'T JUST IGNORING the science—they're actively choosing delusion over data, leaving their kids to pay the price.

~

The Real Victims: Kids Who Don't Get a Say

"You Don't Let a Kid Drive a Car, So Maybe Don't Let Them Rewrite Their DNA."

THE MOST HEARTBREAKING part of this entire fiasco? The kids who grow up realizing their parents made irreversible decisions about their bodies before they were old enough to consent.

Case Study: The Regret Epidemic

MEET SARAH—BORN Samantha. At 11, Sarah's parents fully supported her transition to male, complete with hormone therapy and chest binding. By 18, Sarah realized she didn't want to be male after all, but by then, the damage was done. Her voice is permanently deep, her fertility is gone, and she's left wondering why her parents didn't just let her grow the fuck up first.

REGRET RATES for childhood transitions are rising, but you'll never hear woke parents admit it. They're too busy chasing likes on Twitter to notice the mental health fallout brewing in their own homes.

~

The Hidden Costs of Rushing Decisions

AMID ALL THE satire and insanity, there's a harsh reality that's anything but funny. Take Jason, a 15-year-old whose parents decided at age 8 that he should transition to female because he once said he "felt like a princess." They meant well, wanting to support their child's happiness, but their decision set off a chain reaction of hormone treatments and irreversible surgeries before Jason even hit puberty.

FAST FORWARD TO TODAY: Jason, now identifying as male again, is battling depression and struggling to find his place in a world that doesn't fit the narrative his parents scripted for him. His voice is permanently altered, his body carries scars he didn't choose, and he's left questioning why the people who were supposed to protect him didn't let him just be a kid.

THIS ISN'T AN ISOLATED CASE. Across the globe, kids like Jason are paying the price for decisions they didn't make, carrying the weight of their parents' good intentions gone awry. It's a sobering reminder that childhood is meant for discovery, not experimentation.

~

The Cultural Insanity: From Parental Love to Virtue Signaling

"This Isn't Parenting. It's Fucking Child Abuse."

THE CORE ISSUE here isn't love or support—it's attention-seeking parents projecting their own woke fantasies onto their kids. They're not raising children. They're building woke billboards for the world to applaud.

The Social Media Martyrs

THESE PARENTS CAN'T GO five minutes without posting about their "brave, nonbinary child" and their "progressive journey as allies." The kids? They're props in a never-ending performance, paraded around for clout while their parents rake in likes and sponsorship deals.

The Legal Backlash

What happens when a parent refuses to affirm their child's chosen gender? In WOKE WORLD, it's not just frowned upon—it's criminal. Courts are now stripping custody from parents who hesitate to greenlight hormone therapy or surgeries, declaring them unfit for "not supporting their child's true self."

~

The Social Media Circus: Monetizing Transition for Clout

"Welcome to my channel, where my kid's identity pays the bills!"

IN WOKE WORLD, nothing is sacred—not even your kid's gender. For a growing number of parents, their child's transition isn't just a personal journey—it's a brand opportunity. These woke entrepreneurs treat their kids' identities like a cash cow, milking every hashtag, like, and sponsorship deal they can get.

MEET THE SOCIAL MEDIA MARTYR:

Jessica, a self-proclaimed "progressive pioneer," starts every day by filming her child, Mason—sorry, *Luna*—as they eat cereal in a sparkly tutu. The video goes live with the caption: *"Raising my brave nonbinary butterfly in a world full of hate* 🦋 *#LoveWins #ParentingGoals."*

BEHIND THE SCENES, Luna looks exhausted, asking, "Mom, can I just eat my cereal without being on camera?" But Jessica won't let a good clout moment go to waste. "Just a few more takes, sweetie," she coos, adjusting the rainbow filter.

JESSICA'S TIKTOK followers adore her. They flood the comments with praise:

- "You're such an inspiration!"

- "Luna is so lucky to have you!"
- "Where did you get that tutu?!"

AND SPEAKING OF THAT TUTU, it's part of Jessica's latest sponsorship deal with "WokeWear Kids™"—a clothing brand specializing in gender-neutral glitter overalls and eco-friendly hormone blocker storage cases. Jessica earns a cool $5,000 per post, all while claiming to be *"just a mom trying to make the world better for my child."*

The Rise of the Rainbow Merch Empire:

BUT IT DOESN'T STOP at social media. These parents go full capitalist, launching product lines based on their child's transition. From branded pronoun pins to limited-edition "Trans and Proud" plushies, they turn their kids into walking advertisements. Every birthday party becomes a photo shoot, every milestone an opportunity for a new line of merch.

- One dad released a best-selling children's book, *"Timmy the Brave Seahorse,"* inspired by his child's decision to identify as aquatic. Never mind that Timmy can't read yet—this book is climbing the charts, baby!

- Another mom started a YouTube series, *"Life With Leo (Formerly Lily),"* where she vlogs every step of her son's transition. The channel boasts millions of followers, and the family is now sponsored by a company that makes glitter-infused testosterone gel.

MEANWHILE, the kids are left asking questions like, "Why does my school backpack have my face on it?" and "Do I really have to wear the branded cape to soccer practice?" The parents, however, are too busy counting ad revenue to notice.

The Fallout: Props, Not People

THE REAL TRAGEDY is that these kids aren't seen as individuals—they're props in their parents' never-ending performance of wokeness. Every tear, every triumph, every awkward phase is broadcast to the world for likes and sponsorships. And when the clout dries up? These kids are left with a trail of TikToks, a stack of branded merch, and a gnawing sense that their childhood was just content.

~

The Courtroom of WOKE

"Your Honor, My Child Demands Unicorn Hormones"

PICTURE THIS: a courtroom packed with spectators, journalists, and rainbow flags. At the front, a judge in a sequined robe bangs a glitter-encrusted gavel to call order.

. . .

THE PARENTS, sitting nervously at the defendant's table, are accused of the gravest crime imaginable in WOKE WORLD: *hesitating* to approve their 8-year-old's request for unicorn-themed puberty blockers.

Judge's Opening Statement:

"LADIES AND GENTLEMEN, this is not a case of neglect or abuse. This is a case of **parental bigotry**. By refusing to affirm their child's request to transition into a 'Rainbow Unicorn Being,' these parents have inflicted irreparable harm on their offspring's emotional journey. How dare they deny their child's inherent right to magical puberty blockers?!"

THE PROSECUTION—A SELF-PROCLAIMED "GENDER EMPATHY ALCHEMIST"—STEPS forward to present the evidence. "Your Honor, the defendants committed heinous acts of hesitation. When little Sparkle, formerly known as Timmy, requested a sparkly horn implant and hormone blockers flavored like marshmallows, these so-called parents said they needed 'time to think.' TIME. TO. THINK."

GASPS ECHO THROUGH THE COURTROOM. The spectators, some dressed in unicorn onesies, begin murmuring angrily.

THE PARENTS ATTEMPT to defend themselves. "Your Honor, we just wanted to consult a doctor about the side effects—"

. . .

"SIDE EFFECTS?!" the judge interrupts, their voice dripping with outrage. "Do you hear yourselves? Side effects are just patriarchal propaganda designed to oppress magical beings like Sparkle. I hereby sentence you to mandatory attendance at a three-week Species-Gender Sensitivity Retreat, followed by a year of supervised parenting by a certified Unicorn Advocate."

AS THE GAVEL FALLS, the parents are escorted out of the courtroom, their InclusiVibe apps buzzing with notifications: "BIGOT ALERT: Failure to support child's magical identity. Mandatory empathy training scheduled."

MEANWHILE, Sparkle is handed a golden crown and a plush unicorn horn by the prosecution team, who tearfully declare, "This is justice for all mythical beings!"

~

The Fallout: Broken Kids, Broken Families

THE LONG-TERM CONSEQUENCES of this woke madness are staggering. Kids who transition too early face increased rates of depression, anxiety, and suicide. Families are torn apart by the legal and emotional fallout of decisions made too soon. And society? It's left to pick up the pieces while these parents pat themselves on the back for being "progressive pioneers."

~

Pre-Closing: The Maximum Effort Voice of Reason

LET'S get one thing crystal fucking clear: Maximum Effort doesn't care if you're gay, trans, nonbinary, or a damn unicorn. Your identity is your call, your journey, and your choice. Hell, dye your hair rainbow, slap on some glitter, and be whoever the hell you want to be. That's what freedom is about.

BUT HERE'S the line in the sand: when parents start playing God with their kids' identities—before those kids can spell 'identity,' let alone understand it—that's not progress. That's not love. That's parental narcissism wrapped in woke packaging. It's the adult's need for validation, parading as acceptance, at the cost of a child's future.

KIDS DESERVE the chance to explore who they are without their parents playing damn mad scientist with their future. Childhood is about discovery, not irreversible decisions made before they're old enough to know what irreversibility even means.

IN WOKE WORLD, freedom isn't about choice—it's about compliance. But real freedom? It's letting kids be kids until they're old enough to choose for themselves. Anything less isn't progress. It's lunacy.

THIS ISN'T LOVE. This isn't bravery. It's fucking lunacy wrapped in rainbows, and the ones paying the price are the kids who grow up broken and betrayed. Welcome to WOKE WORLD, where childhood is optional, biology is fake, and parents are the architects of their own damn insanity.

Closing Line: The Ultimate Betrayal

THIS ISN'T LOVE. This isn't bravery. It's fucking lunacy wrapped in rainbows, with a glitter bomb of delusion at its core. The ones paying the price aren't the woke parents basking in Instagram likes —it's the kids growing up broken, confused, and betrayed by the very people who were supposed to protect them. Welcome to WOKE WORLD, where childhood is optional, biology is fake, and parents are the architects of their own damn insanity. May the next generation forgive us—because the current one sure as hell won't.

CHAPTER 6
BOOK REVIEW REQUEST

~

Make a Difference with Your Review

Fuel the Fire, Shape the Narrative

**"Reviews aren't just opinions—they're matches
that ignite the revolution."
– Maximum Effort**

Dear Readers,

Thank you for diving into *WOKE II: The Sequel Nobody Wanted, But Everyone Needs*. We hope this book lit a fire under you, made you laugh until your sides hurt, and gave you the guts to call out the lunacy running rampant today. Your experience with this unapologetic sequel is what keeps the flames burning.

Why Your Review Matters

YOUR REVIEW IS MORE than just words—it's ammo in the fight against the absurdity that *WOKE Nation* first exposed. Sharing your thoughts helps others decide if they're ready to step into the fire of truth and sarcasm. Every review pushes back against the tide of groupthink and gives free thought the platform it deserves.

How to Leave a Review

IT's AS simple as calling out bullshit—quick, bold, and to the point:

1 Click the Book's Review Link:

https://www.amazon.com/review/create-review/?ie=UTF8&channel=glance-detail&asin=B0DRFKBRVC

2 Scan the QR Code:

What to Include in Your Review

- **Your Experience:** Did *WOKE II* challenge you, make you laugh, or piss you off in the best way? Share your reaction.
- **Favorite Sections:** Did a chapter like *Canceling the Cancelers* or *Emotional Support Cactus Nation* hit the mark? Highlight what resonated.
- **The Takeaway:** Did this book confirm your suspicions or completely shift your perspective? Tell us what stuck.
- **Your Verdict:** Let others know why this sequel is the wake-up call they didn't know they needed.

Example Review

"IF YOU THOUGHT Maximum Effort went hard in WOKE Nation, this sequel cranks it up to 11. From the biting sarcasm of The Great Virtue Signal to the relentless takedown of corporate performative wokeness, this book pulls no punches. It's hilarious, infuriating, and brutally honest—

everything we need in a world gone soft. A must-read for anyone tired of tiptoeing around nonsense."

Your Impact

YOUR VOICE MATTERS. Your review doesn't just help this book—it helps a movement. In a world drowning in performative nonsense, your words are a life raft of common sense.

THANK **you** for taking the time to share your thoughts. Your feedback keeps the fire burning and the conversation alive.

WITH RELENTLESS GRATITUDE,

MAXIMUM EFFORT

~

THE PANOPTICON — AI SURVEILLANCE AND MENTAL PRISONS

"Welcome to your padded prison."

~

James had always been a model employee—or so he thought. One Monday morning, he was called into HR. The reason? His heart rate had spiked during a tense meeting, and the AI flagged him for 'hostile tendencies.' By Friday, James was jobless, labeled a 'toxic influence' on team morale. His crime? Having a panic attack under the unblinking eye of empathy AI. He never said a word, but the machines spoke for him.

~

Welcome to the Panopticon

IMAGINE THIS: You wake up, glance at your smartwatch, and it already knows how stressed you are. You grab your phone, and its

AI assistant reminds you of a meeting while subtly judging your sleep patterns. At work, your laptop monitors your keystrokes, your phone tracks your location, and the cameras on your office walls scrutinize every microexpression on your face. This isn't some Orwellian fever dream. This is the world you live in. Welcome to the Panopticon—an AI-powered mental prison where every blink, every twitch, and every glance is being recorded, analyzed, and weaponized against you.

BIG BROTHER ISN'T WATCHING. Big Brother *is* your smartwatch, your phone, and the empathetic AI sitting silently in HR, determining whether your tone was sufficiently supportive during the last Zoom call.

Total Surveillance Culture

YOUR EVERY MOVE IS LOGGED.

EVERY CLICK, every scroll, every swipe—it's all data. That app you downloaded to count your steps? It's also mapping your routines, identifying when you're most likely to skip the gym, and selling that data to advertisers. Your smartwatch doesn't just track your heart rate—it knows when you're anxious, when you're bored, and when you're lying about your calorie intake.

AND AT WORK? Forget about sneaking a glance at your phone or checking Reddit during a meeting. Your employer is already ahead of you. Keylogging software records every word you type. AI-powered webcams analyze your body language during calls. Sensors embedded in office furniture know if you're standing, sitting, or taking too many bathroom breaks. Your productivity, focus, and even "team spirit" are reduced to scores on a dashboard monitored by HR.

The Cost of Convenience

THIS CONSTANT SURVEILLANCE is sold to you as a convenience—something that makes your life "easier." But in reality, it's about control. Control over how you act, what you think, and even how you feel. AI doesn't just want your compliance; it wants your soul. And if you think you can hide, think again. The Panopticon doesn't just watch—it *anticipates*. Algorithms know your habits better than you do, predicting your next move with terrifying accuracy.

$\sim$

Empathy AI: Smile for the Algorithm

EVER HAVE a bad day and just want to be left alone? Too bad. Empathy AI doesn't care about your personal problems. This new breed of workplace surveillance technology is designed to monitor your emotional engagement. Cameras outfitted with facial recognition track every microexpression, scanning your face for signs of dissatisfaction, fatigue, or—God forbid—disagreement during a meeting.

. . .

Dɪᴅ ʏᴏᴜ ꜰʀᴏᴡɴ ᴅᴜʀɪɴɢ ᴀ ᴘʀᴇꜱᴇɴᴛᴀᴛɪᴏɴ? The AI flags you for "low empathy levels." Did you zone out during your boss's monologue about synergy? HR gets a notification that your "team alignment" is slipping. And if you dare to look anything less than thrilled about the mandatory birthday cupcakes in the break room? Congratulations—you've just been labeled a "cultural risk."

Tʜɪꜱ ɪꜱɴ'ᴛ about improving workplace morale. It's about policing emotions. AI doesn't just monitor your behavior; it dictates how you're supposed to *feel*.

Dystopian Scenario:

Iɴ ᴛʜᴇ ᴍᴏꜱᴛ ᴇxᴛʀᴇᴍᴇ ᴄᴀꜱᴇꜱ, workers are outfitted with mood monitors—a patch on their temple that tracks dopamine levels in real-time. If the algorithm detects a 'happiness deficit,' it automatically alerts HR, triggering a mandatory 'wellness intervention.' Failure to 'reset' your mood within the allotted time? That's a formal warning. Too many warnings, and you're out the door. In this world, being stressed isn't just a problem—it's a punishable offense.

Microaggression Sensors: HR's Digital Guillotine

HR ʜᴀꜱ ᴇᴠᴏʟᴠᴇᴅ. It's no longer a department staffed with people awkwardly handing you pamphlets about workplace safety. Now, it's an all-seeing AI overlord equipped with microaggression sensors designed to flag anything and everything that could be deemed "inappropriate."

Your tone of voice during a team call? Flagged for "potential hostility." The way you glanced at a coworker during a meeting? Registered as "subconscious bias." A joke that everyone laughed at but could theoretically offend someone in another universe? Welcome to sensitivity training.

Microaggression sensors don't just police what you say—they police what you *don't* say. Fail to compliment a coworker's idea during a brainstorming session? You're now part of a "toxic workplace culture." Use the wrong tone when saying "good morning"? That's a demerit for "emotional insensitivity." In this world, silence isn't golden—it's damning.

~

The Mental Toll of Constant Surveillance

Living under this digital microscope isn't just invasive—it's exhausting. You're not just managing your work anymore; you're managing your *image*. Every word, every gesture, every pause is calibrated to avoid triggering the AI watchdogs. And the result? Burnout, paranoia, and the slow erosion of genuine human interaction.

You're no longer a person. You're a performer in a dystopian theater, constantly on stage for an invisible audience of algorithms and HR analysts. This isn't a workplace. It's a psychological mine-field where one wrong step could cost you your job—or worse, your sanity.

$$\sim$$

When Compliance Becomes a Cage

THE PANOPTICON ISN'T JUST about surveillance—it's about submission. By tracking your every move, AI creates a culture where conformity is mandatory and dissent is suicidal. You don't question the system because the system knows your questions before you even ask them.

YOU DON'T PUSH BACK because the algorithm has already flagged you as a potential troublemaker.

AND THE WORST PART? You start to police yourself. You smile when you don't want to. You laugh at jokes you don't find funny. You agree with decisions you know are wrong—all because the Panopticon has trained you to prioritize survival over authenticity.

$$\sim$$

The Final Betrayal: You're the Product

AT THE END of the day, this isn't about making you a better employee or improving workplace efficiency. It's about monetizing your existence. Every keystroke, every smile, every glance is data—data that can be sold, traded, or used to manipulate you further. The Panopticon doesn't just watch you. It profits off you. And the more you comply, the more valuable you become.

Closing Line: Every Blink, Every Twitch, Every Glance

EVERY BLINK, every twitch, every glance—they see it all. And the only thing scarier than being constantly watched is realizing you're no longer just a worker, a person, or an individual. You're a statistic in a system that doesn't just want your productivity. It wants your soul. Welcome to the Panopticon—your padded prison in the digital age.

CALL-TO-ACTION:

But what if you pushed back? What if you turned the cameras on the system instead of letting it track you? The Panopticon thrives on compliance, but it crumbles under defiance. Question the algorithms. Demand transparency. Protect your humanity, even when the machines try to strip it away. The padded prison only wins if you forget there's a world outside its walls.

IN THE PANOPTICON, you don't just lose your privacy—you lose the right to be human.

CHAPTER 8
CLOUT CHASERS — HOW OUTRAGE BECAME A CAREER PATH

"Nothing's funny anymore. Everything's offensive."

~

Pull back the curtain on Clout Chasers — bounty hunters of outrage who profit from takedowns, cancellations, and public apologies. This chapter exposes their playbook, reveals their motivations, and highlights why Maximum Effort never bows to their demands.

~

Clout Chasers as Modern-Day Bounty Hunters

CLOUT CHASERS OPERATE like bounty hunters, but instead of chasing criminals, they hunt for "problematic content" to expose and profit from.

- **Hunting for Cancelable Offenses** — Clout Chasers scan old tweets, TikTok clips, livestreams, and Facebook photos, looking for anything they can weaponize.
- **The Bounty System** — The bigger the target, the bigger the reward. Celebrities, influencers, and brands are the "whales" Clout Chasers love to harpoon.

How They Select Their Targets

- **Trending Traps** — They wait for someone to trend, then dive into their past to find old "offensive" content.
- **Doomscroll Dredging** — Clout Chasers scour old MySpace profiles, 2012 tweets, and archived livestreams to dig up "evidence."
- **Bad Take Bait** — They bait targets into responding to controversial "hot takes," waiting for one slip-up to pounce.

"They're not hunting for justice — they're hunting for jackpots. And you're the bounty."

Monetizing Outrage — The Clout Chaser Business Model

OUTRAGE ISN'T RANDOM. It's profitable. Clout Chasers monetize every stage of the takedown process, from viral callouts to apology tours.

- **Sponsorships & Brand Deals** — Once they build a following, brands like "Do Better Soap Co." and "Accountability Coffee" pay them to be "ambassadors of justice."
- **Reaction Videos** — They film "live reactions" to apology videos, milking them for YouTube, TikTok, and Instagram ad revenue.
- **Donation Grifts** — Chasers drop Venmo and CashApp links, claiming "the emotional toll of canceling people is hard on my mental health."
- **Cancel Merch** — Merch with slogans like **"Do Better"** and **"Hold Them Accountable"** are sold for profit.
- **Apology Economy** — The more viral an apology goes, the more cash Clout Chasers make. They clip, share, and react to every groveling sob story.

"Outrage isn't random — it's a business model. And Clout Chasers are cashing in."

Anatomy of a Clout Chase — How They Manufacture Outrage

Every Clout Chase follows a predictable playbook — here's how it's done, step-by-step.

1. **Spot the Target** — Wait for someone to trend, get attention, or make headlines.
2. **Dig for Dirt** — Search old tweets, past livestreams,

Reddit threads, and even old yearbook quotes for "problematic content."

3. **Trigger the Callout** — Post the screenshot with the iconic caption **"So this you?"**
4. **Tag Big Players** — Tag big influencers, media accounts, and "callout warriors" to increase exposure.
5. **Fuel the Fire** — Use buzzwords like **"Hold Them Accountable," "This is unacceptable,"** and **"We Demand an Apology"**.
6. **Monetize It** — Drop donation links, reaction videos, and sponsorships for "justice work."
7. **Repeat the Cycle** — Move to the next target and repeat.

"It's not about justice. It's about timing. The quicker they 'find your dirt,' the quicker they secure the bag."

The Rise of the Clout Chaser Hero Complex

CLOUT CHASERS SEE themselves as "heroes of justice" fighting for accountability, but they're really after fame, clout, and brand deals.

- **The Savior Syndrome** — Clout Chasers frame themselves as selfless "protectors of the vulnerable," but in reality, they're fishing for sponsorships.
- **Weaponizing Empathy** — They claim to care about justice and empathy, but they milk every apology for profit.

· · ·

How They Spin The Narrative: The 3-Act Clout Chaser Playbook

Clout Chasers use a predictable, repeatable storyline for every "takedown." If you've seen one, you've seen them all. Here's how it plays out:

Act 1: The Call to Action

"I just HAD to say something..."

This is where the Clout Chaser sets the stage for their "hero's journey." They frame themselves as the only person brave enough to "call out injustice" — as if millions of other people on the internet don't already have Twitter fingers locked and loaded. **This is the 'main character moment' they've been waiting for.**

Key Tactics in Act 1:

- **The "Reluctant Hero" Setup** — They act like they didn't *want* to do this, but they just "couldn't stay silent anymore," *"Look, I wasn't even going to say anything... BUT..."*

- **The 'I'm So Brave' Flex** — They hype themselves up as a "whistleblower," painting themselves as a lone soldier fighting injustice. *"I know I might get backlash for this, but I have to speak up."* (They won't. They'll get sponsorships.)

- **Planting Empathy Seeds** — They make it seem like they're protecting "the vulnerable" or "speaking up for the voiceless." *"Some of y'all might not understand why this matters, but marginalized communities are counting on me to expose this."* (Translation: "Like, comment, and share my video.")

Real-World Scenario (Act 1):

- Clout Chaser spots a TikTok of a mom packing her kid's lunch.
- Clout Chaser tweets: *"I wasn't going to say anything, but why are there only TWO fruit options? Are we not discussing how food deserts affect this?!?!"*
- Their followers start replying with "This!! Shit" and "Yesss. Finally, someone said it!" The Chaser now has the "moral high ground" and the dopamine rush of validation.

"They claim to be 'reluctantly brave,' but they've been drafting that callout tweet for three days straight."

. . .

Act 2: The Callout

"Y'all see this, right??"

THIS IS THE BIG MOMENT. The Clout Chaser has the "receipts" and they're about to "bravely expose" their target. This moment is **all about the screenshot.** You know the one — blurry, 1.5x zoom, covered in red circles like a Madden playbook.

Key Tactics in Act 2:

- **The Screenshot Bombshell** — The grainy, pixelated, slightly zoomed-in screenshot of an old tweet, TikTok clip, or livestream moment that "proves" the villain's guilt. *"So THIS you?"* (The caption that launched 1,000 cancellations.)

- **Use of Red Circles & Highlights** — Red circles are drawn around irrelevant details that *look* damning but mean nothing. Screenshot of a Tweet with "2012" circled like it's a clue on a murder board.

- **Tagging Big Players** — This is where they tag accounts like @CallOutJustice, @OutrageDaily, and popular Clout Chasers to boost the exposure. *"Hey*

@CallOutJustice, do you see what I see??" (They see it. They always see it.)

- **Use of "Viral Buzzwords"** — Phrases like: **"Unacceptable." "This is why we need to talk about X." "DO BETTER." "I'm literally shaking."**

Real-World Scenario (Act 2):

- Clout Chaser finds a celebrity's old tweet from 2010 that says, *"Just watched Twilight. Team Edward for life, lol."*

- Clout Chaser takes a blurry screenshot, zooms in, circles "Edward," and captions it with: *"We're not gonna talk about how they supported a relationship with a 100-year-old predator? Y'ALL SEE THIS SHIT, RIGHT??"*

- **Instant explosion.** Replies flood in: *"Omg, cancel them."* *"I knew they were problematic."* Clout Chaser's engagement goes through the roof.

"If you see a blurry screenshot with red circles,

run. It's not evidence — it's a content creator chasing clout."

Act 3: The Public Praise

"I'm just so happy people are finally listening."

THIS IS THE VICTORY LAP. The Clout Chaser has successfully "exposed" the villain-gained followers, and now they're basking in the glow of **retweets, donations, and sponsorship offers.** Their follower count spikes. Their inbox is full of "partnership inquiries" from "social justice brands" like **Accountability Coffee Co.** and **Cancel Culture Candles.**

Key Tactics in Act 3:

- **Retweeting Praise** — Every compliment, every "Yassss king" comment, every "You're doing the Lord's work" gets retweeted for maximum validation.Clout Chaser Quote-Tweets: *"Thank you so much for seeing me. It means everything."*

- **Public Victory Lap** — They post a "reflective" selfie with captions like:*"I'm just so grateful that I was able to use my platform to create change."* (They'll do it again tomorrow.)

. . .

- **Donation Grift** — They add a CashApp or Venmo link with: *"Canceling takes a toll on my mental health. If you feel led to support me, here's my link."* (Translation: *I made $6K today for dragging someone.*)

- **Partnership Flex** — They post their new "ambassador" deal with **Do Better Soap Co.** or **Clout Chaser Energy Drinks.**

Real-World Scenario (Act 3):

- After "exposing" the 2010 "Team Edward" tweet, the Clout Chaser now tweets: *"I just want to thank y'all for supporting me. I didn't expect to get 15K new followers, but I'm ready to use my platform for GOOD."*

- Donations roll in. They buy a new gaming chair.

"They frame it as 'healing from emotional exhaustion,' but somehow they have the energy to drop their CashApp in the comments."

. . .

"They're not heroes. They're bounty hunters. And their bounties are your past mistakes."

~

Real-Life Case Studies — The Worst Clout Chasers in History

REAL-WORLD EXAMPLES of Clout Chasers gone wild. These are the most infamous and ridiculous moments in Clout Chaser history.

- **Case Study 1: TikTok Mob vs. Small-Town Bakery —** Yelp review attack after a bakery didn't update its logo for Pride Month.

- **Case Study 2: The 10-Year-Old Tweet —** A comedian is "canceled" after Clout Chasers dig up a joke from 2012.

- **Case Study 3: Twitch Apology Factory —** A Twitch streamer is forced to "apologize" for a joke from 8 years ago. Chasers react, monetize it, and cash out.

- **Case Study 4: Corporate Apology Clown Show —** Brands like Bud Light and Target get bullied into issuing "public apologies" — and Clout Chasers cash in on the spectacle.

- **Case Study 5: The Emoji That Canceled a Career** — A person posts a " 💀 " emoji under a celebrity's post. Clout Chasers twist it into a "death threat" and trigger a full-scale cancellation.

- **NEW Case Study 6: The 'Laugh React' that Launched a Thousand Outrages**

"LMAO = Label Me A Oppressor"

If you thought emojis were dangerous, wait until you hear about **"The Laugh React Cancellation."** This one? This one will make you **rage-tweet on behalf of humanity.**

The Setup:

A high school senior named Maya was scrolling Facebook. Her aunt posted a "motivational quote" about *"Rising Above Your Haters"* with a generic stock image of a person climbing a mountain. It was the kind of post people scroll past every day. No big deal, right?

Well, Maya hit " 😂 " **(laugh-react)** on the post by accident. It happens to everyone. Maybe her thumb slipped. Maybe she thought it was funny in an ironic way. Maybe she didn't even realize she did it. The problem? Her aunt didn't see it that way. And her aunt's friends? Oh, they had time.

The Callout:

By the time Maya checked her phone that night, she had **53 comments** on the laugh-react. Most of them were from her aunt's friends. Some highlights:

- **"Care to explain what's so funny, Maya?"**
- **"We really thought you were better than this."**
- **"You're laughing at black women trying to rise up?"**

That last comment set it off. Someone screenshot the 😂 reaction, circled it in red (of course), and posted it in a Facebook group called **"Accountability Watch"** with the caption:

"This is why Gen Z has NO RESPECT for older generations."

By morning, Maya's name was posted on **"The Accountability List"**, a public document shared in several private Facebook groups. **Her phone blew up.** One DM even read:

"Apologize now before we contact your college admissions office."

The Fallout:

- **Her School Counselor Got Involved:** She was called into the counselor's office to discuss the "incident" and was told that "microaggressions, even unintentional ones, can have real consequences."

- **College Admissions Threatened:** Two Clout Chasers found out she had been accepted to **NYU**, so they tagged NYU Admissions on TikTok saying:

"Y'all accepting people like THIS???"

- **Facebook Apology Tour:** Under pressure from her parents, Maya posted a long, teary-eyed apology on Facebook that began with:

"I now see how my laugh-react was harmful. I was ignorant of how others might view it. I promise to educate myself and do better."

- **Donation Grift:** Clout Chasers filmed themselves **"reacting" to her apology**. They posted TikToks saying, *"She doesn't mean it. This is just a PR move."* and included **CashApp links** in the captions.

The Aftermath:

Her NYU application was placed "Under Review" for two weeks. The admissions office eventually cleared her, but her mental health didn't recover for months.

Her family spent $600 on therapy. Maya deleted all social media.

She now calls herself **"The Laugh React Girl"** in every college essay she writes.

. . .

“One laugh-react on a stock photo post, and this girl was nearly blacklisted from NYU.”

"If your company logo doesn't turn rainbow-colored during June, Clout Chasers will see you in digital court."

~

The Maximum Effort Manifesto — Why We Never Chase Clout

MAXIMUM EFFORT DOESN'T CHASE clout. We chase greatness. Clout Chasers are parasites feeding off validation, while Maximum Effort is too busy building empires. This is the ultimate "mic drop" moment — a declaration of independence from the outrage economy.

EMPOWER the reader to break free from the clout addiction that's ruining lives, draining mental energy, and keeping them stuck in an endless loop of apology, shame, and self-censorship. **This is the rebellion call.**

Step 1: Log Off — They Can't Cancel What They Can't Find

"The only way to win a rigged game is to stop playing."

THE CLOUT CHASERS can't cancel you if they can't see you. The second you log off, the algorithm stops tracking you, Clout Chasers lose their target, and outrage has nowhere to land.

HOW TO DO IT:

- **Unfollow the Noise:** Mute, block, and unsubscribe from drama-chasing pages, clickbait media, and outrage accounts.
- **Delete Old Bait:** Clean up old social media accounts where Clout Chasers might "Doomscroll Dredge" for content to use against you.
- **Digital Minimalism:** If you're not building a business or brand, why are you even online? Delete the apps that don't serve your goals.
- **Kill Notifications:** Notifications are mini dopamine traps. Turn them off, and your peace returns.

WHY IT WORKS:

- Outrage depends on the audience. If you log off, you're no longer the audience. Clout Chasers need you to engage, like, comment, and retweet. If you **log off**, they lose their power.
- Clout Chasers can't "So This You?" someone who isn't active online. They have no screenshots, no ammo, and no target.

"Clout Chasers scream for attention. The quietest person in the room is the only one they can't cancel."

Step 2: Never Apologize to Strangers — They Don't Care

"If they don't know you, they don't deserve an apology."

THE BIGGEST MISTAKE people make is apologizing to people they've never met. Clout Chasers **don't want your apology — they want your submission.** The second you bend the knee, they own you. Stop apologizing to strangers. Stop explaining yourself to people who don't care about you. **Stop playing their game.**

HOW TO DO IT:

- **Ask This Question Before Apologizing:** "Does this person know me? Do I care about them?" If the answer is no, Fuck 'em, the apology is unnecessary.
- **Set a Hard Rule:** "I do not apologize to strangers." If you have to, pin this rule to your phone's lock screen.
- **Recognize the Trap:** Clout Chasers will say, "Just apologize, and it'll all go away." It's a trap. They will never accept your apology.

WHY IT WORKS:

- Clout Chasers **don't care about apologies**. They only care about controlling you. The second you apologize, they'll demand more.
- Public apologies fuel Clout Chasers' content. Reaction videos, "breakdowns" of your apology, and donation grifts start the second you hit "post."

"Apologizing to strangers is like throwing blood in shark-infested waters. They don't swim away — they swarm."

Step 3: Apologize once. Burn the script. Use the ashes to roast marshmallows.

"Apologize once. No repeats. No rewrites."

APOLOGIES HAVE BECOME a twisted public spectacle. People are pressured to "apologize better" or "apologize the right way" — and every time they apologize, Clout Chasers demand more. **Stop the madness cycle.** Apologize once (only if absolutely necessary), and move on. **If they don't accept it, that's their problem, not yours.**

HOW TO DO IT:

- **Keep it Short:** "I'm sorry for [X]. I'm working to be better." End it there. No need for a novel. No 3-minute apology videos. No follow-ups.

- **Post It and Ghost It:** Once you post an apology, turn off comments. Walk away. You owe them nothing more.
- **No Double Apologies:** If they don't accept your first apology, **do NOT re-apologize.** Their goal is to keep you apologizing forever.

Why It Works:

- Clout Chasers thrive on prolonged apologies. They want "apology tours" because it gives them content for their next video. By **apologizing once and disappearing**, you kill their supply.
- Apologizing once shows strength. **Re-apologizing shows weakness.** Clout Chasers smell weakness like blood.

"Apologies are a single-use item. Use it once, burn the script, and never read from it again."

Maximum Effort Rules for Living Clout-Free

THIS IS where we lay out **The Rules** for readers to print, memorize, and live by. This could be printed as a "wall poster" moment in the book. These rules should feel like commandments for people trying to escape clout culture.

. . .

THE 7 RULES OF MAXIMUM EFFORT LIVING

1. **Log off. They can't cancel what they can't find.**
2. **Never apologize to strangers. They don't care.**
3. **Apologize once. Burn the script. Walk away.**
4. **Ignore Clout Chasers — They scream louder when you're silent - Sit back and laugh.**
5. **Silence is power. Engagement is weakness.**
6. **Don't argue with fools. It only proves there are two.**
7. **They chase clout. You chase greatness.**

"Clout Chasers chase validation. Maximum Effort chases victory. The difference is everything."

~

Closing Line

"You can apologize, cry, and beg for forgiveness — or you can burn the apology script, toss on some shades, and walk away. The mob never forgets, but it sure as hell gets bored."

"Never wrestle with pigs. They love the mud, and you end up dirty."

"Don't feed the trolls — and never, ever feed the Chasers."

CHAPTER 9

THOUGHTCRIME —
BANNED WORDS AND THE
END OF FREE SPEECH

"One wrong word, one wrong thought, and you're erased."

∿

Welcome to the Language Gulag

Imagine this: you wake up, pour yourself some coffee, and check your work email. The first notification? A cheerful HR reminder: *"Friendly notice! The word 'boss' is now deemed hierarchically insensitive. Please refer to your boss as your 'Team Impact Facilitator.' Failure to comply will result in mandatory Re-education Training."*

You shrug it off, thinking this can't get any more ridiculous. But by lunchtime, Slack has flagged your message—"I'll loop in my boss"—and HR is calling. "You've been flagged for hierarchical aggression," they say. By dinner, you're sitting in a virtual seminar titled *"Deconstructing Linguistic Privilege in Corporate Culture."*

WELCOME TO THOUGHTCRIME, where free speech is a relic, every word is a potential landmine, and you're one misplaced comma away from being un-personed. This isn't just censorship—it's a damn language lobotomy brought to you by the overlords of woke HR.

Banned Words of the Day: Yesterday's OK, Today's Offense

EVERY DAY, the list of forbidden words grows longer, more ridiculous, and infinitely more confusing. What was perfectly acceptable yesterday is today's equivalent of yelling "Fire!" in a crowded theater. The corporate language overlords don't just ban words—they rewrite the rules of engagement, leaving everyone scrambling to decode the latest *Vocabulary Compliance Memo*. And trust me, it's a shitshow.

HERE'S AN EXPANDED SAMPLER of the linguistic landmines now deemed unacceptable, along with their corporate-approved replacements:

AND LET'S not forget the phrases that get flagged for violent imagery. Words that were once tools of expression are now treated like weapons of mass destruction. A few offenders:

Gendered Language

WORDS AND PHRASES deemed problematic for their gendered connotations:

- **"Guys"**: Deemed sexist and exclusionary. Use "team," "folks," or the robotic "all." Slip up once, and you'll be fast-tracked to the Gender-Neutral Language Sensitivity Seminar.
- **"Man hours"**: Out for obvious reasons. Replace with "person hours" or "effort hours," even if it makes you sound like a robot.
- **"Manpower"**: Also banned. Use "workforce" or "human resources" as if HR hasn't already taken enough from your soul.

Ableist Terminology

PHRASES CONSIDERED offensive for referencing physical or mental abilities:

- **"Blindspot"**: Allegedly marginalizes individuals with visual impairments. Use "knowledge gap." Heaven forbid you metaphorically admit to missing something.
- **"Walk-in"**: Considered ableist since not everyone can "walk." Use "drop-in," even if the person physically walked through the door.
- **"Lame"**: Out. Apparently, you meant "unfortunate." Slip up, and HR is already drafting your reprimand.

- **"Crazy" or "Insane"**: Stigmatizing mental health. Use "wild" or "unexpected." But keep it measured—too much enthusiasm could trigger the enthusiasm police.

Cultural Appropriation

PHRASES FLAGGED for borrowing from or misrepresenting cultures:

- **"Spirit animal"**: Cultural appropriation alert! Use "inspiration" or "guide" instead.
- **"Powwow"**: Off-limits as it appropriates Indigenous traditions. Opt for a "team huddle" or "informal meeting," even if it kills the vibe.
- **"Eskimo kiss"**: Considered insensitive to Inuit peoples. Use "nose bump," though it somehow sounds worse.
- **"Trap House"**: Offensive for perpetuating stereotypes. Replace it with "abandoned building" or "illicit residence" because drug dealers definitely care.

Historically Insensitive Phrases

TERMS with alleged problematic origins or connotations:

- **"Grandfathered in"**: Ageist, historically insensitive, and patriarchal. Use "legacy policy." Bonus points if you don't cry from boredom while saying it.
- **"Rule of thumb"**: Allegedly rooted in myths about domestic violence. Say "general guideline."

- **"Cakewalk"**: Racist origins. Replace with "easy task," though it won't make finishing the task any easier.
- **"Peanut gallery"**: Associated with segregated seating in theaters. Use "hecklers" or "commentators," though neither has the same charm.
- **"Call a spade a spade"**: Historically problematic. Use "be direct" or "tell it like it is." Or just don't talk.

Workplace-Inspired Replacements

Phrases scrubbed for being too violent, outdated, or otherwise unacceptable:

- **"Brainstorm"**: Offensive to neurodivergent individuals. Use "thought shower." If that phrase feels like being waterboarded by HR, congratulations— you're human.
- **"Low-hanging fruit"**: Considered disrespectful to metaphorical trees and agricultural workers. Use "easy win" or "quick fix."
- **"Take a stab at it"**: Too violent. Say, "Give it a try."
- **"Kill two birds with one stone"**: Out. Use "feed two birds with one scone." Yes, scone—because apparently, imaginary pigeons deserve better.
- **"Deadline"**: Too morbid. Use "due date" or "target date" instead.

Pop Culture Casualties

NAMES OR SLANG phrases that don't survive HR's linguistic purge:

- **"Karen"**: Mentioning this name, even jokingly, gets you sent to the Respect for All Names Workshop.
- **"Kinda Gay"**: Dismissed for trivializing LGBTQ+ identities. Say "exploring identity," or avoid the phrase altogether.
- **"Gay"**: Strictly context-dependent. "Joyful" for traditional use or "LGBTQ+ individual" for modern contexts. Misuse invites mandatory Language Inclusivity Training.

Catch-All Creativity Killers

METAPHORS AND DESCRIPTORS treated like weapons of mass destruction:

- **"Killing it"**: Too violent. Say "doing great" or "excelling." Apparently, metaphors are scary now.
- **"Black sheep"**: Considered exclusionary. Say "unique contributor" because outcasts just need better PR.
- **"Nitpick"**: Offensive to people with obsessive tendencies. Use "focus on details." HR swears overthinking is perfectly inclusive.

Absurdly Specific Changes

PHRASES where the replacements are as ridiculous as the bans:

- **"Brown bag"**: Allegedly racist. Use "lunch and learn." No word on whether clear bags are more inclusive.
- **"Crusade"**: Too religious. Replace with "campaign" or "initiative." Just don't offend medieval historians.
- **"Trap House"**: Offensive. Say "abandoned building" or "illicit residence" because euphemisms fix everything.

THIS EVER-EXPANDING list doesn't just limit language—it annihilates creativity. Every word you say is one step closer to offending someone somewhere. As this linguistic circus continues, it's only a matter of time before we're all reduced to grunting in fear. But hey, at least it'll be "inclusive."

The Hypocrisy of the Orwellian Bakery

EVEN HARMLESS PHRASES that evoke humor or culture are under siege. Want to tell someone to "roll with the punches"? Nope. Too violent. How about "low-hanging fruit"? Sorry, it's disrespectful to metaphorical trees and possibly agricultural workers.

AND YET, the corporate overlords have no problem replacing these "harmful" words with their own branded jargon. Need a moment to collect your thoughts? Don't bother saying, "I need a minute." Instead, try, "Let me ideate asynchronously." That's right—HR expects you to sound like a human thesaurus while simultaneously gutting your personality.

~

The Reality of Linguistic Whack-a-Mole

THE ABSURDITY of banning these words isn't just laughable—it's unsustainable. Language evolves organically, but the Thoughtcrime regime operates like a linguistic whack-a-mole game. The second you adapt, the goalposts move:

- Yesterday's "acceptable" term—"diversity"—is today's "problematic buzzword." HR now prefers "multidimensional inclusivity."
- "Cultural fit"? Problematic. Try "values alignment."
- "Hard work"? Too aggressive. Opt for "dedicated effort."

THE RESULT? A never-ending cycle of re-education that drains morale, creativity, and, let's face it, any remaining will to live.

What the Fuck Can We Even Say?

AT THIS POINT, you might be wondering: *What's left?* If every word is a potential offense, what's the secret to surviving this linguistic minefield? The answer? Utter blandness. Strip your vocabulary down to the safest, most lifeless expressions possible. Welcome to the age of corporate beige, where creativity dies, and every word feels like it was pulled from an HR compliance manual.

Your Crash Course in Corporate Beige: How to Speak Without Saying Anything

1. **Neutral Greetings**: Forget "Hey guys" or "Good morning, team." Stick to the sterile, all-encompassing "Hello, all." Or, better yet, skip words entirely. Just nod vaguely in the direction of your coworkers and hope they interpret it as friendly, not passive-aggressive.

2. **Universal Praise**: Think "Great job, Karen" is safe? Think again. You'll end up in the "Respect for All Names" seminar before you can say, "Karen isn't even offended." Instead, go with, "Wonderful effort, colleague." It's generic, lifeless, and guaranteed to offend absolutely no one—except, maybe, your soul.

3. **Emotion-Free Feedback**: Replace "I loved your idea!" with "Your contribution aligns well with our objectives." Sure, it sounds like it was written by a malfunctioning chatbot, but at least HR won't accuse you of favoritism or bias.

4. **Non-Offensive Humor**: Humor? Don't even think about it. But if you *must* attempt a joke, keep it as safe as possible: "That's mildly amusing." Say it with a straight face and immediately follow it with, "This is not intended as sarcasm," just in case.

5. **Conflict Resolution**: Forget saying, "Let's tackle this issue." Instead, try, "Let's address this opportunity for alignment." Nobody understands what it means, but it sure *sounds* non-confrontational.

6. **Requests for Help**: Don't say, "I need assistance with this project." Go with, "I'd appreciate your collaborative input." It's vague enough to make your coworker guess what you need, sparing you the risk of sounding too direct.

Now, Imagine:

EVERY CONVERSATION TURNS into a parody of itself. Every email reads like it was written by an AI program terrified of offending the algorithms that created it. Every interaction becomes a lifeless, monotone exchange of sanitized phrases that strip away any hint of personality, humor, or humanity.

YOU WANT TO COMPLIMENT SOMEONE? You better make it sound like you're reading a script. Do you want to express frustration? Forget it. Venting is now classified as "emotional insensitivity." Do you want to say something witty to lighten the mood? HR is already preparing your pink slip.

IN THIS DYSTOPIA, the only safe communication is silence. But wait—that could be interpreted as disengagement, which might flag you for a lack of team spirit. Congratulations—you're damned if you do and damned if you don't.

The Real Kicker

EVEN IF YOU master this soul-crushing game of linguistic Twister, you're not safe. The second you adapt to one set of "safe" phrases, the goalposts move. Today's "acceptable" is tomorrow's "offensive." It's a linguistic arms race where the only certainty is that you'll eventually lose.

. . .

Let's say you memorize the latest Vocabulary Compliance Memo. You stop saying "guys" and start saying "team." You drop "brainstorm" in favor of "thought shower." You survive the Thoughtcrime Tribunal by nodding along to every ridiculous rule. You think you're in the clear. Then, out of nowhere, HR declares that "thought shower" is now ableist because not everyone enjoys showers. Back to square one.

So, What the Fuck Can We Even Say?

Here's the answer: **Nothing.** Every word is a risk. Every phrase is a liability. Every conversation is a potential HR tribunal waiting to happen. Silence might seem like the safest bet—but even that can be misinterpreted as disengagement, disrespect, or passive aggression. The truth is, we're all one slip-up away from our linguistic funeral.

Focus Question:

"So, really, what the fuck can we say anymore? If every word is a potential offense and every thought is a liability, is silence the only option left? Or are we just waiting for the day when even thinking the wrong thing gets us flagged by HR's Mind-Reading AI?"

~

Absurdity Check: How Did We Get Here?

How did expressing yourself become a minefield of bureaucratic buzzwords? Somewhere along the line, corporate America decided that words—not systemic inequality, not toxic leadership, not the crushing weight of late-stage capitalism—were the real problem. And instead of addressing those real issues, they slapped a censor on language, called it "progress," and patted themselves on the back.

But here's the kicker: the more words they ban, the more convoluted and meaningless communication becomes. At this rate, we'll all be reduced to nodding silently and gesturing like Sims.

The Price of Compliance

The cost of this insanity isn't just annoyance—it's freedom. Freedom to express yourself. Freedom to disagree. Freedom to, dare I say it, make a joke without worrying if the algorithms are listening. And let's be real: if HR keeps banning words at this rate, we'll need a damn AI translator to make it through the day.

So, next time you're about to say something, remember: the walls have ears, the AI has eyes, and your vocabulary has consequences. Choose your words carefully—or better yet, don't choose them at all.

Because in this world, silence isn't just golden—it's fucking mandatory.

~

HR Thought Audits: Policing the Mind, One Slack Message at a Time

Do you think you can vent privately to a coworker? Think again. Every Slack message, every email, every damn emoji is monitored by AI-powered Sentiment Analysis Tools™. These algorithms scan for "problematic sentiment," flagging anything that could be interpreted as hostile, negative, or (the ultimate sin) sarcastic.

Case in Point:

LAST WEEK, a junior designer named Rachel replied "👍" to her manager's message about mandatory weekend overtime. The AI flagged her for "passive-aggressive behavior." HR scheduled her for a *"Collaborative Attitude Workshop."*

AND IT GETS WORSE. These tools aren't just looking for bad words—they're analyzing tone. Send an email that's too curt? You're flagged for "emotional insensitivity." Express doubt about a new company initiative? That's "non-alignment with organizational goals." Try cracking a joke. Forget it. Humor is a liability in the world of Thoughtcrime.

~

Vocabulary Compliance Tests: Speak or Be Silenced

EVERY MONTH, employees at Thoughtcrime Inc. are required to take the *Vocabulary Compliance Test*. It's like a spelling bee from hell, except instead of spelling words, you're memorizing the latest HR-approved phrases. Here's how it works:

- You're given a series of scenarios and asked to pick the "inclusive" response.
- Choose incorrectly, and you're immediately flagged for *"non-compliance."*
- Three strikes, and it's off to *"Language Re-education Training."*

EXAMPLE QUESTION:

Scenario: A coworker asks if you want to "brainstorm" ideas. What do you say?

A. "Sure, let's brainstorm!"
B. "Let's have a thought shower instead!"
C. "Actually, let's synergy our ideations collaboratively."

THE CORRECT ANSWER? *B,* obviously. Option **A** will get you flagged as a linguistic dinosaur, and Option **C** will earn you points for effort but still fail for using jargon without HR pre-approval.

The Thoughtcrime Tribunal

GET FLAGGED TOO MANY TIMES, and you'll find yourself in front of the Thoughtcrime Tribunal—a three-person HR panel armed with binders full of your offenses. They'll review your "case file," which includes:

1. Slack transcripts (yes, they keep them all).
2. Sentiment Analysis Reports (you were "too negative" during Q2).
3. Audio clips from meetings (your sigh during that diversity training didn't go unnoticed).

THEIR DECISION? Re-education, demotion, or termination. The tribunal's motto: *"We don't punish. We rehabilitate."* Which sounds a lot like punishment when your next job title is *"Assistant to the Regional Compliance Liaison."*

～

The Psychological Toll of Word Policing

LIVING under constant linguistic surveillance does more than stifle free speech—it fucks with your head. You're not just thinking about what to say; you're agonizing over how to say it, whether it'll be misinterpreted, and if it'll cost you your job. The result? A workplace where nobody says anything remotely authentic, and conversations devolve into robotic platitudes.

～

Signs You're in a Thoughtcrime Zone:

- You spend five minutes drafting a two-sentence Slack message.
- You avoid talking in meetings altogether.
- You find yourself apologizing for things you haven't even said yet.
- You feel a pit in your stomach every time HR sends a "friendly reminder" email.

THIS ISN'T JUST CENSORSHIP—IT'S psychological warfare. The Thoughtcrime regime doesn't just silence you. It makes you silence yourself.

~

The Final Betrayal: Free Speech Is Dead, Long Live Compliance

AT ITS CORE, Thoughtcrime isn't about fostering inclusion or creating safe spaces. It's about control. By banning words, monitoring thoughts, and punishing dissent, the Thoughtcrime regime ensures that everyone speaks in unison—even if nobody believes a damn word they're saying.

AND THE IRONY? In trying to protect people's feelings, they've destroyed the one thing that makes us human: the ability to speak freely, disagree passionately, and, yes, sometimes offend each other.

~

Closing Line: The Only Safe Words

The only safe words in Thoughtcrime aren't "please" or "thank you." They're "I'm sorry" and "I agree." Everything else is a risk. So choose your words carefully—or don't choose them at all. In this world, silence isn't just golden. It's mandatory.

~

Corporate Beige Survival Kit

Closing Section:

The Corporate Beige Survival Kit™

Still, struggling to navigate the linguistic hellscape of modern corporate life? Fear not! The *Corporate Beige Survival Kit™* is here to save your sanity (or what's left of it). Guaranteed to help you dodge Thoughtcrime tribunals and HR's all-seeing eye, this satirical set includes:

- **The Corporate Buzzword Bingo Card:** Transform your misery into fun by marking off terms like "synergy," "alignment," and "values-driven innovation" during every soul-sucking meeting. Just don't shout "Bingo!"— it could be interpreted as aggressive enthusiasm.
- **HR-Approved Dictionary:** A pocket-sized book of pre-approved phrases with strict context notes, so you'll never accidentally offend someone by saying "brainstorm" again. Includes updates like "thought sprinkle" for when "thought shower" becomes problematic.
- **Emotionally Neutral Email Templates:** Need to reply to a coworker without risking HR intervention?

Templates like "Thank you for your input, colleague" or "I appreciate your collaborative spirit" are guaranteed to keep you in the linguistic clear.

- **The Silence is Compliance Mug:** A reminder that in today's workplace, it's safer to sip than to speak. Bonus: It's insulated for those long, mandatory diversity seminars.
- **Pre-Apology Sticky Notes:** Write "I'm sorry" in advance to save time. Stick them everywhere—on your desk, your laptop, your forehead—because you're going to need them.

Solution or Final Mockery:

LET'S BE HONEST—NO survival kit can save you from this Orwellian nightmare. The only way to truly win this game is not to play. But until corporate sanity is restored (**spoiler: it won't be**), you can at least laugh while you quietly grieve the death of free expression.

OR, if you're feeling bold, ditch the beige altogether and fight back by saying the most dangerous phrase of all:

> **"Why don't we just talk like normal human beings?"**

JUST MAKE sure HR isn't listening.

WOKE II

CHAPTER 10

UNPERSONED — DIGITAL ERASURE AND SOCIAL DEATH

"Delete the account. Delete the person. Delete the history."

~

Imagine waking up one morning to discover that you no longer exist—not legally, not digitally, not even socially. Your phone vibrates with a barrage of notifications—but instead of messages, they're error alerts. The Uber app stutters before flashing, 'Account not found.' You fumble to check PayPal, only to find an ominous red banner: 'This account has been permanently disabled.' Your heart races as Gmail refuses to load, locking you out with an innocuous-sounding, 'Couldn't verify your account.' By the time you realize your Venmo is inaccessible, a sinking feeling settles in your chest. You try calling customer support, but the automated voice greets you with, 'We have no record of this account. Your Uber app doesn't work. PayPal says your account doesn't exist. Venmo insists you're not real. It's not a glitch. It's your punishment. This is digital erasure, the twenty-first-century death sentence. In the

157

corporate panopticon, where your every click and scroll is monitored, being *Unpersoned* is the final punishment.

~

The New Frontier of Punishment: Digital Death Sentences

FOR CENTURIES, societies punished with exile, stripping individuals of their place in the community. But in today's hyper-connected world, exile isn't a physical act; it's digital annihilation. With a single keystroke, the systems you depend on—financial, logistical, social—can evaporate.

UBER WON'T PICK you up, no matter how urgently you need a ride. PayPal and Venmo? Gone, along with every dollar they held. Netflix? Forget binging—your account is wiped, and with it, every recommendation you've ever curated. Even your Gmail stops loading. You've been *Unpersoned*.

~

What Does Digital Erasure Look Like?

1. Financial Annihilation

THE FIRST TO GO IS ALWAYS YOUR money. Your bank apps suddenly reject your credentials. PayPal shows an error message: *"Account not found."* Credit cards are frozen. You're cut off from your assets—instant poverty in the most humiliating way. Try explaining to your landlord that Venmo erased your rent payment or to the grocery clerk that your debit card worked fine yesterday.

. . .

2. Social Erasure

Next, your online presence vanishes. Facebook? Deactivated. Instagram? The account doesn't exist. LinkedIn? Profile removed. It's as if you never existed. The ripple effect is brutal: friends can't find you, family assumes the worst, and colleagues quietly drop you from professional networks. In a world where your social footprint is your identity, this is a kind of digital death.

3. Logistical Limbo

Need a ride to work? Uber and Lyft say you're not registered. Want to order dinner? DoorDash and Grubhub claim your address isn't valid. Even Amazon, the behemoth that knows everything about everyone, greets you with *"We can't find your account."* You're left stranded, hungry, and disconnected, a ghost in a machine that no longer recognizes you.

❧

The Mechanisms of Erasure

How does it happen? Simple: a network of systems that were supposed to make your life easier now work in perfect harmony to erase you.

1. AI and Algorithms

THE VERY ALGORITHMS designed to recommend your next favorite show or suggest a playlist now flag you as non-compliant. An Uber driver reports your behavior as "suspicious"? That's enough to lock you out. A PayPal transaction gets misread as fraudulent. Goodbye, funds.

2. **Corporate Collusion**

ONCE ONE PLATFORM decides you're a problem, the others follow suit. Your accounts are linked across services, so when one goes, they all do. The same system that connects your apps to your email to your credit card now orchestrates your erasure.

3. **No Due Process**

THE SCARIEST PART? There's no trial. No warning. No appeal. One moment, you're part of the digital ecosystem; the next, you're erased. The only notification you'll receive is a generic *"Your account has been permanently disabled."*

~

The Psychological Toll

DIGITAL ERASURE ISN'T JUST a logistical nightmare—it's a psychological one.

1. **Isolation and Alienation**

- Humans are social creatures. When your online presence disappears, you lose more than convenience—you lose connection. Friends wonder if you blocked them. Employers think you've ghosted them. It's a social death spiral.

2. **Loss of Identity**

- In a world where your digital accounts are an extension of yourself, their loss feels like amputation. You're not just losing access; you're losing pieces of who you are.

3. **Paranoia and Fear**

- After being Unpersoned, every click feels risky, every login precarious. The system that erased you once could do it again, for any reason—or no reason at all.

❧

Case Studies in Digital Death

1. **The Freelancer's Nightmare: Alex**

ALEX'S ALARM jolted her awake. She groggily reached for her phone to check emails from clients, but her Gmail app refused to load. Anxiously, she switched to her PayPal account, only to be greeted with the chilling error message: *"Account not found."* Panic set in. Her clients' payments—gone. Rent was due in two days, and she had no way to access the money she'd already earned.

. . .

Desperate, Alex called her best friend. *"Can you PayPal me the rent? I'll figure out how to repay you later."* The friend tried, but Alex's account was permanently disabled. She suggested Venmo, but that account had vanished too. Within 24 hours, Alex was borrowing cash just to keep her phone connected—her lifeline to a career that no longer existed.

2. The Social Pariah: Jordan

For Jordan, digital erasure wasn't just an inconvenience—it was a death sentence for their activism. After years of building a community on Twitter and Facebook, their accounts were erased overnight following a post flagged as "hate speech." The post? A criticism of corporate environmental practices.

Without their network, Jordan was forced to retreat to obscure platforms with names like "Connect.Me" and "SocietySphere," where engagement was minimal and spam bots made up half the user base. The funding for their latest project dried up as their donors assumed they'd disappeared. In less than a week, Jordan went from being a respected voice in their community to an echo in a forgotten corner of the internet.

3. The Average Joe: Sam

Sam's day started like any other until his Uber driver misunderstood his frustration over traffic as *"aggressive behavior."* Sam received an email from Uber later that day: *"Your account has been suspended due to a violation of our community guidelines."* Annoyed but undeterred,

Sam tried to switch to Lyft, but his account there was flagged too—linked to the same phone number and payment information.

THE NEXT MORNING, Sam woke up to find his Venmo and Spotify accounts locked. Without a ride, he had to walk five miles to work. He arrived late, sweaty, and exhausted, only to be met with his boss's disapproval. *"This is unacceptable, Sam. If it happens again, we'll have to let you go."* By the end of the week, Sam wasn't just Unpersoned—he was unemployed.

~

Can You Come Back from Being Unpersoned?

SHORT ANSWER: no. The system isn't designed to forgive or forget. Attempts to create new accounts are flagged and blocked. Even your IP address might be blacklisted.

SOME TRY to rebuild their digital lives with burner phones and prepaid credit cards. Others give up entirely, retreating to an analog existence. But in a society where everything from job applications to medical records is digital, the odds are stacked against you.

~

The Bigger Picture: Who Decides?

WHO DECIDES that you're unfit for the digital world? It's not a judge or jury. It's an algorithm—a faceless, soulless code designed to enforce policies it doesn't even understand.

. . .

EVEN SCARIER IS the power these corporations hold. With no oversight, they've become judge, jury, and executioner. They don't just control access; they control existence.

Closing Line

"YOU'VE BEEN UNPERSONED. No bank, no Uber, no Netflix. You don't exist."

IN THIS WORLD, the final punishment isn't jail—it's erasure. And the scariest part? You'll never see it coming.

BEING Unpersoned isn't just the loss of convenience—it's the loss of everything that makes modern life functional. The scariest part isn't the act of erasure—it's the realization that it can happen to anyone at any time, for any reason. In a world where algorithms judge, platforms execute, and society forgets, the final punishment isn't prison or exile—it's disappearance. And once it happens, there's no coming back.

CHAPTER II

BURN IT ALL DOWN

"Stay, apologize, and cry forever. Or leave it all behind."

∼

The decision is yours. Stay in the system that chews you up, spits you out, and demands your gratitude—or torch it. Burn the bridges. Burn the system. Burn the chains that bind you.

THIS ISN'T JUST about survival anymore. It's about rebellion. It's about reclaiming what you've lost, what they took from you, and what you were too afraid to demand back. This is your line in the sand. Stay, apologize, and cry forever—or burn it all down and never look back.

∼

The Cost of Compliance: How Woke World Keeps You Enslaved

Let's face it: compliance isn't just exhausting; it's soul-destroying. Every apology chips away at your identity. Every "diversity training" meeting dulls your fire. Every censorious rule keeps you tethered to a system that feeds off your silence.

Staying Means:

1. **Living on Your Knees**

You'll beg for scraps of approval from HR overlords who see you as nothing more than a liability. Your once-bright individuality will fade into a gray sludge of compliance, stripped of humanity, creativity, and courage.

2. **Apologizing for Existing**

You'll master the art of self-censorship, constantly policing your thoughts, words, and actions. Even your most innocent intentions will feel like sins under the crushing weight of groupthink.

3. **Crying Forever**

Because no matter how hard you try, you'll never be perfect enough. The rules will always shift. The goalposts will always move. And when they do, they'll remind you: *This is your fault.*

. . .

STAYING MEANS SLOW DEATH. Not of the body—but of the spirit.

The Explosive Alternative: Burn It All Down

BURNING it down isn't chaos—it's liberation. It's not about abandoning the world but rebuilding your place in it on your own terms. To burn it all down is to dismantle the chains they've wrapped around you and use the flames to light your path forward.

HERE'S HOW:

Step One: Stop Apologizing

Every apology feeds the machine. Every "I'm sorry" is a tiny surrender. It's time to stop being a Pussy.

- **Own Your Intentions**: If you meant no harm, stand by your words. Explain, but don't grovel. Apologizing for simply existing only deepens their control.

Example: Instead of saying, "I'm sorry if my comment upset you," say, "That wasn't my intention, but I stand by my point."

- **Redefine "Accountability"**: Understand the difference between genuine accountability and performative apology. Be accountable for real mistakes, not for offending fragile egos.

- **Celebrate Imperfection**: Perfection is their leash. Be unapologetically flawed and human. The moment you stop striving to meet their impossible standards, you start reclaiming your freedom.

Step Two: Log Off

Logging off doesn't mean vanishing—it means regaining control. The digital world thrives on your constant participation. Opt-out.

1. **Declutter Your Digital Life**:

- Identify apps and platforms that drain your energy or feed your fear. Delete them.
- Keep tools that empower you or bring authentic connection. Everything else? Let it burn.

2. **Audit Your Social Media Usage**:

- Limit your screen time and turn off notifications.
- Use social media intentionally: connect with people, not outrage. Share your truth, not your curated highlight reel.

. . .

3. **Invest in Real-World Connections:**

- Replace endless scrolling with tangible actions—call a friend, join a local community, or pursue a hobby you've been neglecting. The real world has more to offer than likes and retweets.

Step Three: Reclaim Your Life

REBUILDING after burning it down isn't just about survival—it's about thriving.

1. **Speak Freely Without Fear:**

- Practice speaking your truth in small, safe environments first. Build the courage to expand your voice.
- Surround yourself with people who value honest dialogue, not performative virtue signaling.

2. **Take Back Your Time:**

- Replace time spent on performative activities (e.g., endless meetings or superficial networking) with pursuits that enrich your life.
- Set boundaries with work, social obligations, and digital

intrusions. Your time is yours—treat it like the precious resource it is.

3. **Redefine Success on Your Own Terms:**

- Break free from the corporate ladder's definitions of achievement. Success isn't titles or approval—it's living a life aligned with your values.
- Celebrate small wins and build a life rooted in authenticity, not validation.

What to Expect After Burning It Down

Burning it down comes with challenges, but the rewards far outweigh the risks:

1. **Challenges:**

- You may lose connections with people who don't understand your choices.
- Some opportunities might close, but they're likely ones that didn't serve you anyway.

2. **Rewards:**

- **Clarity**: Without the noise of digital clutter, you'll discover what truly matters to you.
- **Freedom**: No more walking on eggshells or censoring yourself to meet someone else's expectations.
- **Confidence**: You'll learn to trust your instincts and live without constantly seeking external approval.

Your Burning Toolkit

To ensure you're prepared for this journey, equip yourself with these tools:

- **A Core Group of Allies**: Find a small, trusted group of people who share your values and will support you in your rebellion.
- **A Clear Mission**: Define what you're walking away from and, more importantly, what you're walking toward.
- **A "Hell No" List**: Write down what you'll no longer tolerate—whether it's toxic environments, pointless apologies, or exhausting digital habits.

Take Action Now

The world will tell you to wait. To keep your head down. To stay small. Don't.

- Uninstall the app that drains you the most.

- Have one real conversation where you speak your truth, uncensored.
- Write down one dream you've been putting off and take the first step toward it—today.

BURNING IT DOWN IS A JOURNEY, not a one-time act. It's a decision you make every day: to reject what doesn't serve you and build something that does.

REBELLION ISN'T EASY, but it's worth it. The chains you break today will pave the way for a future where you live unapologetically, authentically, and joyfully. So take the matches they gave you—and start the fire.

~

What Happens When You Burn It Down?

FREEDOM HAS A COST. Walking away from Woke World might mean losing friends, followers, and even opportunities. But what you'll gain is worth more than anything you could ever lose:

- **Your Voice**

WHEN YOU STOP FILTERING your thoughts through layers of fear, your voice becomes powerful. People won't just hear you—they'll listen.

- **Your Time**

No more wasted hours on pointless meetings, performative apologies, or scrolling through outrage. Your time becomes yours again.

- **Your Life**

Without the constant pressure to conform, you'll rediscover who you are—and who you're meant to be.

∼

For the Brave Few: A Manifesto for the Burn-It-All-Down Generation

To the brave few, this is your call to arms. This is your anthem. This is your moment to rise.

We are the ones who refuse to be silenced.

We are the ones who choose defiance over compliance, courage over comfort, and authenticity over acceptance.

The system will try to break you. It will crush you under the weight of conformity, drown you in empty apologies, and chain you with fear. But you are not their pawn. You are not their puppet. You are not their prisoner.

. . .

You are the fire they cannot extinguish.

- **We will not apologize for existing.**

WHEN THEY DEMAND an apology for the crime of being yourself, you will stand tall and say, "No." No to their guilt. No, to their shame. No to their relentless attempts to make you smaller.

- **We will not censor our thoughts to fit your narrative.**

YOUR MIND IS YOUR OWN. Your thoughts are your sanctuary. Speak them loudly, boldly, and unapologetically—even if it shakes the world around you.

- **We will not trade our humanity for your approval.**

THEIR APPROVAL IS A LEASH, and you were born to run free. Refuse to bow to a system that thrives on stripping you of your individuality.

- **We will speak boldly, live fully, and burn brightly.**

BE the match that lights a thousand fires. Be the spark that ignites change. Be the flame that reminds the world what it means to live unapologetically.

. . .

THIS ISN'T JUST REBELLION—IT'S revolution. It's a movement of the brave, the bold, the unapologetically human.

> *When they try to silence us, we will roar.*
> *When they try to shame us, we will stand.*
> *When they try to erase us, we will burn brighter*
> *than ever.*

TO THE BRAVE few who dare to burn it all down:

YOU ARE NOT ALONE. You are part of a generation that refuses to be enslaved by fear. You are part of a rebellion that will not be extinguished. You are part of a revolution that begins with you.

> *This is your fire. This is your freedom. This is your*
> *fight.*

Rallying Cry:

- When they tell you to conform, **shatter the mold.**
- When they tell you to stay silent, **speak louder.**
- When they tell you to obey, **burn it all down.**

THIS IS YOUR REVOLUTION. Your rebellion. Your time to rise. Let your fire light the way for others who are still trapped in the shadows.

. . .

Closing Declaration:

> "We will not bow. We will not break. We will burn with a fire so bright it will outlive the system that tried to silence us. This is the beginning. This is our time. This is the age of the brave few."

~

Final Call to Action

The time for hesitation is over. This isn't just a chapter in a book; it's the turning point in your life. You've seen the machine for what it is—a soul-crushing, joy-stealing, identity-erasing monstrosity. You can either continue feeding it with your apologies and compliance, or you can stand up, take back your power, and set the whole damn thing on fire.

This is your moment. Not tomorrow. Not next week. Now.

- **Stop apologizing for existing.**
- **Log off and live your truth.**
- **Speak boldly, even when it shakes the foundations of their fragile system.**

Refuse to be a cog in their machine. Refuse to play their game. Refuse to live your life in grayscale when you were born to shine in technicolor.

. . .

Burn it all down. Not with violence but with defiance. Not with chaos but with clarity. Not with fear, but with fire—the fire of your courage, your freedom, and your unrelenting refusal to conform.

You've read the words. You've felt the anger, the frustration, the suffocating weight of their rules. Now it's time to act. Stand tall, breathe deeply, and light the match.

This is your rebellion. **This is your revolution. This is your life.**

"Stay, apologize, and cry forever—or burn it all down and never look back. The choice is yours. Choose freedom."

~

EPILOGUE: MAXIMUM EFFORT'S SURVIVAL GUIDE FOR WOKE II: THE SEQUEL NOBODY WANTED, BUT EVERYONE NEEDS

Congratulations, you've survived *WOKE II* without getting canceled, joining a cult of emotional support houseplants, or punching a hole through your monitor. That alone makes you a badass among sheep. In a world where every fart is a microaggression, every thought is a landmine, and every opinion has to pass through the Ministry of Offense, you've proven you have the grit to stand tall while the rest of the world bows down.

BUT LET'S BE REAL: surviving this shitstorm isn't a passive act. It takes strategy, sarcasm, and a big, shiny pair of metaphorical balls. So, buckle the hell up because this isn't just another survival guide—it's a masterclass in rebellion.

Survival Rules for WOKE II: The Fucking Shitshow

Rule #1: Laugh at the Lunacy

WHEN SOMEONE PETITIONS TO ban the sun for being "too aggressive," don't argue—laugh. And I'm not talking about a polite chuckle. I mean, laugh so loudly and obnoxiously that Karen's yoga mat rolls itself up in shame. The minute you take this circus seriously, you've lost. Humor is your flamethrower in a world full of snowflakes.

Rule #2: Know When to Shut Up

NOT EVERY BATTLE is worth fighting. Sometimes, the best way to win is to let the lunatics run their asylum. The next time someone tweets that oxygen is problematic because it disproportionately benefits humans, don't engage. Save your energy for meaningful fights, like pineapple on pizza or whether Die Hard is a Christmas movie.

Rule #3: Create a Bingo Card of Bullshit

SURVIVING *WOKE II* IS A MARATHON, not a sprint. Make it fun. Turn the nonsense into a game. Every time you see something absurd, mark it off your card. A few gems for your starter pack:

- Emotional support cactus on an airplane.
- Gender-neutral pronouns for the moon.
- Outrage over the "oppression" of bananas being peeled.
- Someone calling peanut butter "violent" because it "dominates" jelly.

IF YOU HIT Bingo by Wednesday, reward yourself with a stiff drink. Hell, reward yourself anyway—you've earned it.

The Official Maximum Effort Survival Playbook

Step 1: Stop Apologizing

EVERY "I'M SORRY" is another brick in their wall of bullshit. Quit playing their game. If you offended someone, own it—or better yet, double down.

- Did you call someone "guys" instead of "team"? Good.
- Did you question their sacred ideology? Excellent.
- Did you post a meme that made someone cry? Perfect.

THEIR TEARS ARE NOT your problem. Be unapologetically you, because bending the knee only gets you kicked in the face.

Step 2: Ditch the Digital Circus

WOKE WORLD FEEDS on your digital breadcrumbs—likes, clicks, and outrage shares. Cut off their food supply.

1. **Purge the Toxic Crap**: Delete apps that make you hate humanity. Start with Twitter. Trust me, it's a cesspool of whining and virtue-signaling.

. . .

2. **Reconnect with Reality**: Go outside. Talk to real people. Find someone who doesn't care about hashtags or pronouns and have a conversation that doesn't involve performative outrage.

3. **Use Social Media to Troll, Not Comply**: If you must stay online, make it count. Post memes, call out hypocrisy, and enjoy the chaos. Just don't take it seriously—it's all a game.

Step 3: Burn It Down and Rebuild

BURNING it down isn't about destruction—it's about liberation. It's about saying, "Fuck this noise," and creating your own rules.

1 RECLAIM YOUR Voice

- Stop walking on eggshells. Say what you mean, mean what you say, and let the chips fall where they may. If someone's offended, hand them a box of tissues and tell them to write their therapist.

2 BUILD a Tribe of Real Ones

- Find people who get it. The ones who laugh at the absurdity instead of crying into their kale smoothies. Build a circle of unapologetic, brutally honest, gloriously offensive friends who have your back when the mob comes for you.

3 REDEFINE SUCCESS

- Screw their metrics. Likes, shares and follower counts are meaningless. Success is living life on your terms without apologizing for who you are or what you believe.

Maximum Effort's Manifesto: For the Brave Few

TO THE REBELS, the cynics, and the unapologetically real: this is your battle cry.

- **We refuse to bow.** To the HR overlords, the thought police, and the professionally offended—fuck your rules. We'll speak our minds, laugh at your absurdity, and live our lives without your permission.

- **We reject your narrative.** We won't be boxed in by your guilt, your shame, or your never-ending list of banned words. Our thoughts are ours, and you can't have them.

. . .

- **We embrace chaos.** Life is messy, offensive, and gloriously imperfect. We won't sanitize it for your comfort.

- **We fight back with laughter.** Sarcasm is our weapon, and we wield it with precision. Every joke, every roast, every sarcastic retort is a middle finger to your fragile utopia.

Final Words: The Ball's in Your Court

YOU'VE SEEN THE CIRCUS. You've survived the sequel. Now the choice is yours: stay silent, play nice, and cry yourself to sleep—or join the rebellion.

START SMALL. Call out bullshit when you see it. Laugh at the absurdity. Live your life so unapologetically that Karen breaks out in hives whenever she hears your name.

THIS ISN'T JUST SURVIVAL—IT'S war. And in this war, your greatest weapon is your refusal to conform. Be loud. Be bold. Be the unrelenting pain in their ass that reminds them not everyone will fall in line.

Final Rallying Cry

To the brave few who dare to stand tall in Woke World:

- Speak your truth, even if it shakes the room.
- Live your life, even if it pisses them off.
- Burn it all down, and never look back.

Congratulations, you've survived WOKE II: The Sequel Nobody Wanted, But Everyone Needs. Now go forth and prepare for *WOKE III*, because you know it's coming.

And if they don't like it? Well, they can kindly go fuck themselves.

∾

CHAPTER 12

BOOK REVIEW REQUEST

~

Make a Difference with Your Review

Fuel the Fire, Shape the Narrative

**"Reviews aren't just opinions—they're matches
that ignite the revolution."
– Maximum Effort**

Dear Readers,

Thank you for diving into *WOKE II: The Sequel Nobody Wanted, But Everyone Needs*. We hope this book lit a fire under you, made you laugh until your sides hurt, and gave you the guts to call out the lunacy running rampant today. Your experience with this unapologetic sequel is what keeps the flames burning.

Why Your Review Matters

YOUR REVIEW IS MORE than just words—it's ammo in the fight against the absurdity that *WOKE Nation* first exposed. Sharing your thoughts helps others decide if they're ready to step into the fire of truth and sarcasm. Every review pushes back against the tide of groupthink and gives free thought the platform it deserves.

How to Leave a Review

IT'S AS simple as calling out bullshit—quick, bold, and to the point:

1 Click the Book's Review Link:

https://www.amazon.com/review/create-review/?ie=UTF8&channel= glance-detail&asin=BODRFKBRVC

2 Scan the QR Code:

What to Include in Your Review

- **Your Experience:** Did *WOKE II* challenge you, make you laugh, or piss you off in the best way? Share your reaction.
- **Favorite Sections:** Did a chapter like *Canceling the Cancelers* or *Emotional Support Cactus Nation* hit the mark? Highlight what resonated.
- **The Takeaway:** Did this book confirm your suspicions or completely shift your perspective? Tell us what stuck.
- **Your Verdict:** Let others know why this sequel is the wake-up call they didn't know they needed.

Example Review

"If you thought Maximum Effort went hard in WOKE Nation, this sequel cranks it up to 11. From the biting sarcasm of The Great Virtue Signal to the relentless takedown of corporate performative wokeness, this book pulls no punches. It's hilarious, infuriating, and brutally honest—

everything we need in a world gone soft. A must-read for anyone tired of tiptoeing around nonsense."

Your Impact

YOUR VOICE MATTERS. Your review doesn't just help this book—it helps a movement. In a world drowning in performative nonsense, your words are a life raft of common sense.

THANK **you** for taking the time to share your thoughts. Your feedback keeps the fire burning and the conversation alive.

WITH RELENTLESS GRATITUDE,

MAXIMUM EFFORT

BIBLIOGRAPHY

American Psychological Association. (2021). *Guidelines for inclusive language in communication*. APA Style. https://apastyle.apa.org/inclusive-language

Dawkins, R. (2006). *The god delusion*. Houghton Mifflin Harcourt.

Kaufmann, E. (2019). *Whiteshift: Populism, immigration, and the future of white majorities*. Abrams Press.

Lukianoff, G., & Haidt, J. (2018). *The coddling of the American mind: How good intentions and bad ideas are setting up a generation for failure*. Penguin Books.

Maximum Effort. (2024). *WOKE Nation, Broke Nation, Joke Nation: One nation under woke, divided by idiocy*. Maximum Effort Publishing.

Maximum Effort. (2024). *WOKE II: The sequel nobody wanted, but everyone needs*. Maximum Effort Publishing.

National Public Radio. (2020, July 14). *From "safe spaces" to "trigger warnings": A look at the evolution of woke culture*. NPR. https://www.npr.org/2020/07/14/safe-spaces-and-trigger-warnings

Pinker, S. (2018). *Enlightenment now: The case for reason, science, humanism, and progress*. Viking.

Politico. (2021, September 15). *Cancel culture: The new battlefield in American politics*. Politico. https://www.politico.com/cancel-culture

Sowell, T. (1993). *Inside American education: The decline, the deception, the dogmas*. Free Press.

Thompson, D. (2021, April 7). *The rise and fall of outrage culture*. The Atlantic. https://www.theatlantic.com/outrage-culture

Weiss, B. (2021). *How to fight back against cancel culture*. The New York Times. https://www.nytimes.com/cancel-culture

ABOUT THE AUTHOR

Maximum Effort is not here to hold your hand or stroke your ego. He's the brutal, unfiltered voice of the resistance against today's tidal wave of idiocy, and he's not pulling any punches. With a pen that cuts deeper than your HR compliance manual and a wit sharper than your ex's passive-aggressive texts, Maximum Effort has become the go-to authority for those who refuse to drink the Kool-Aid of modern absurdity.

As the unapologetic mastermind behind **WOKE Nation, Broke Nation, Joke Nation, and WOKE II: The Sequel Nobody Wanted, But Everyone Needs,** Maximum Effort has made a career out of torching bullshit, demolishing hypocrisy and turning the dumpster fire of contemporary culture into literary gold. His books and journals are a rallying cry for anyone who's fed up, pissed off, and ready to laugh at the insanity of it all.

When he's not dismantling the latest corporate buzzwords or canceling cancel culture, Maximum Effort is busy perfecting his whiskey-fueled rants, curating the world's most epic sarcasm bingo cards, and hosting underground snark fests that would make HR cry. His hobbies include roasting societal stupidity, banning the word "problematic," and refusing to apologize for his existence.

Follow Maximum Effort on social media (if you can handle it) or explore his unapologetic catalog on Amazon. But don't say we didn't warn you—his brilliance might just offend your delicate sensibilities. If you're ready to stop apologizing, start thinking, and laugh your ass off while burning it all down, Maximum Effort is your guy.

PSA: No safe spaces were harmed in the making of this bio, but if you're triggered, he suggests pairing your outrage with a stiff drink and a sense of humor.

www.ingramcontent.com/pod-product-compliance
Lightning Source LLC
Chambersburg PA
CBHW051602250726
48653CB00004BA/1289